# The Emergence of the Urban Entrepreneur

# The Emergence of the Urban Entrepreneur

## How the Growth of Cities and the Sharing Economy Are Driving a New Breed of Innovators

Boyd Cohen, PhD, with Pablo Muñoz, PhD

*Foreword by Richard Florida*

## PRAEGER™

An Imprint of ABC-CLIO, LLC

Santa Barbara, California • Denver, Colorado

**Library of Congress Cataloging-in-Publication Data**

Names: Cohen, Boyd, author.
Title: The emergence of the urban entrepreneur : how the growth of cities and the sharing
   economy are driving a new breed of innovators / Boyd Cohen, PhD, with Pablo Muñoz, PhD ;
   foreword by Richard Florida.
Description: Santa Barbara, California : Praeger, [2016] |
   Includes bibliographical references and index.
Identifiers: LCCN 2015051350 | ISBN 9781440844553 (hardcopy : alk. paper) |
   ISBN 9781440844560 (ebook)
Subjects: LCSH: Urban economics. | Entrepreneurship. | Urbanization—Economic aspects.
Classification: LCC HT321 .C576 2016 | DDC 330.9173/2—dc23
LC record available at http://lccn.loc.gov/2015051350

ISBN: 978–1–4408–4455–3
EISBN: 978–1–4408–4456–0

20  19  18  17  16      1  2  3  4  5

This book is also available as an eBook.

Praeger
An Imprint of ABC-CLIO, LLC

ABC-CLIO, LLC
130 Cremona Drive, P.O. Box 1911
Santa Barbara, California 93116-1911
www.abc-clio.com

This book is printed on acid-free paper ∞

Manufactured in the United States of America

# Contents

# Foreword

Long ago, in her book *The Economy of Cities*, Jane Jacobs told the story of Ida Rosenthal, the Russian-born seamstress who opened a dress shop in New York City in 1921. To make her customers' dresses fit better, she devised a new kind of undergarment that she called the Maidenform bra.

Rosenthal wasn't a solitary genius; she was a classic entrepreneur in the mold of a Thomas Edison or Steve Jobs. Her husband, William, and her partner, Enid Bisset, played a huge role in the development of the product, but Ida connected the dots, orchestrating all of the people and processes that went into the creation of not just the bra but the brand. Place played a big role, too. In New York, Rosenthal had ready access to investors who knew the rag trade, to engineers and managers who knew how to set up and run efficient manufacturing processes, to retailers and the countless middlemen and distributors who understood the supply chain, and to advertisers and marketers who helped her create the iconic advertisements that were as innovative as her bras.

When it comes to entrepreneurship, a great city like New York is a giant petri dish. Thanks to its diversities of people and industries, it is crowded with creative people who are smart and ambitious; thanks to its densities, they are forever rubbing up against each other, sparking new ideas and inventions—and then marshalling the skills, the capital, and the networks that are needed to build them into successful economic enterprises.

But until recently, high technology was the great suburban exception to the urban rule. Pioneering companies like Hewlett Packard, Digital Equipment, Intel, and Fairchild Semiconductor all arose along Boston's Route 128 or in the Bay Area's Silicon Valley, as did Apple and Google in the 1970s and 1980s. Microsoft was in Redmond, outside Seattle;

Dell was in suburban Austin. Back in the 1980s, when Martin Kenney and I were studying the geography of venture capital, we could not identify a single urban center that housed a significant cluster of high-tech innovation and venture capital–backed start-up activity.

It was a real conundrum. If cities were such nonpareil engines of innovation, how was it that the most innovative and fastest-growing industry of all mostly thrived outside them? For all that Jane Jacobs wrote about the urban "mingling of diversity," high-tech nerdistans, with their endless tracts of detached houses, had a cookie-cutter sameness to them.

That question has effectively been rendered moot over the past decade and a half as start-ups and high-tech industry have flooded back into urban centers and walkable suburbs. San Francisco now tops Silicon Valley by a wide margin as the United States' and the world's leading center for start-up activity and venture capital investment. New York City has overtaken Boston as the world's second leading center for start-ups and venture capital. It is happening all over the globe. London, Berlin, Paris, Amsterdam, Dublin, Madrid, and Barcelona in Europe; Toronto, Montreal, and Vancouver in Canada; Bangalore, New Delhi, and Mumbai in India; Singapore and Sydney in the Asia Pacific region; and Buenos Aires and Rio de Janeiro in Brazil have all emerged as high-tech start-up centers.

Why the change? Largely because talent demands it. "Technology innovation doesn't occur in a vacuum. It happens in a dialog with society," the New York venture capitalist Fred Wilson memorably blogged. "[T]hat's one of the reasons that many of the most interesting bay area start-ups are choosing to locate themselves in the city. And it is one of the reasons that NYC is developing a vibrant technology community. Society is at its most dense in rich urban environments where society and technology can inspire each other on a daily basis."[1]

It's also due to changes in technology. A generation or so ago, established companies and start-ups alike mostly developed proprietary software systems, designed and manufactured chips, built computers, and laid down the infrastructure that made the Internet possible. For that, they needed big teams, and they needed the big spaces that suburban office parks provide to house them.

Today's fastest-growing companies are more likely to be developing social media, games, music, and retailing applications; they need designers and composers and writers and marketers as much as they do engineers, and cities have more diverse skillsets and talent than most nerdistans can supply. At the same time, cloud-based applications allow start-ups to work with much smaller teams; they can afford the rents on smaller urban spaces—or utilize the incubators and coworking spaces that are popping up in urban creative districts.

Most likely, the old suburban nerdistan was simply a historical aberration that occurred because high tech arose in parallel with the suburbs and urban flight. The rise of urban tech is less a startling reversal than a correction, a return to normalcy. But as Boyd Cohen shows in these pages, it's not just the "why" of urban tech that's so interesting and important but the "what" of it. The new generation of urban entrepreneurs, to turn a phrase, "Think Different" than the last one did. "Urbanpreneurship," Cohen argues, turns on a different set of values than the ones that built Silicon Valley and Route 128.

With the rise of crowd funding and the Minimum Viable Product idea, urbanpreneurs are less dependent on venture capital and venture capitalists' outsized expectations for scalability. The pursuit of patents and the ruthless protection of intellectual property are no longer the keys to the kingdom either. As open-source models and collaboration increase in importance, the "sharing economy" is becoming a genuine ethos. Companies like Airbnb and Uber are not only making billions of dollars for their creators, but are also creating opportunities and even building community.

For all their daunting problems of inequality and race and poverty, for all their current and past struggles with pollution, de-industrialization, and crime, on the one hand, and unaffordability and gentrification, on the other, our cities are our greatest engines of economic, social, and cultural progress. Urbanpreneurship is more democratic, more green, and more civic minded than what came before. Its leaders are not just creating new industries, but changing the way we live and working to solve some of our most pressing challenges. *The Emergence of the Urban Entrepreneur* provides a probing, thoughtful, and genuinely hopeful glimpse into a brave new world of urban innovation.

> —Richard Florida, Director of the Martin Prosperity
> Institute of Toronto's Rotman School of Management,
> Global Research Professor at New York University,
> cofounder and editor-at-large of *The Atlantic*'s CityLab,
> and author of the best-selling book
> *The Rise of the Creative Class*

# Preface

In 1995 I was enrolled in a master's program in Human Resources at the University of South Carolina (USC). Perhaps because USC has always had a world-class reputation in international business, I became intrigued by international business affairs and decided to complete my master's degree in Copenhagen Business School. This was after completing an internship with Accenture, the global consultancy, in Atlanta.

After studying for my last semester in Copenhagen and traveling (maybe a little too much) to cities throughout Western Europe, I returned to the United States to begin working as a change management consultant in Accenture's Denver office. Three years later I began my PhD at the University of Colorado in strategy and entrepreneurship. The first ever academic research project I was involved with was a study of the entrepreneurial ecosystem in Boulder, Colorado, and the neighboring tech parks. Boulder's entrepreneurial ecosystem has already been covered in numerous research projects and was the inspiration for Brad Feld's 2012 book, *Startup Communities*.

As I was finishing my PhD, one of my advisors suggested I read the book *Natural Capitalism*, by Paul Hawken, Amory B. Lovins, and L. Hunter Lovins, which sought to demonstrate that established companies and entrepreneurs could actually profit by embracing environmental and social sustainability. At the time, the idea was pretty revolutionary and the book was a big success. This mindset framed the next decade of my academic career and also served as the starting point to several green start-ups I launched in Vancouver, from consulting to software and mobile technology.

In 2009, I began work on my first book, *Climate Capitalism*, which was written with Hunter Lovins, a co-author of *Natural Capitalism*.

Following a similar approach, we sought to illustrate the business case for
the low-carbon economy across several key industries from energy and
buildings to transportation and food. The book was published in 2011
and by then I had already turned my attention to cities. Perhaps this is
not surprising given the fact that by 2011, I had already lived in
Atlanta, Boulder, and Denver, Copenhagen, Madrid, and Vancouver.
I was increasingly frustrated with the slow pace of international action
on climate change and recognized that cities held the power to act more
quickly to reduce emissions and support low-carbon economies. Cities
are home to a majority of the world's population, are by far the largest
sources of carbon emissions and energy consumption, but also are home
to growing amounts of innovators and entrepreneurs, and are often led
by entrepreneurial mayors such as Vancouver's Gregor Robertson and
Michael Bloomberg, who recently left New York City's highest office.

In 2011 I began studying the emerging trends around smart cities in
places like Amsterdam, Barcelona, Boston, Vienna, and Singapore.
I developed a tool for benchmarking and ranking smart cities called the
Smart Cities Wheel. I have leveraged this tool to publish rankings of
smart cities in *Fast Company* since 2011.

As you can see in Figure 0.1, the Smart Cities Wheel takes quite
a holistic view of what smart cities are, with a focus on the economy,
environment, smarter government, smarter living, smarter mobility, and
smart people. Along with the main categories and their subcomponents,
I have worked on developing a series of indicators to measure smart cities
in more depth. I am regularly asked to reflect on what smart cities actually
are. For me the easiest way to desribe the complexity of a more holistic
view of smart cities is to say that smart cities are innovative cities. They
are innovative in the use of technology, including increasing use of
e-government for service delivery and the implementation of sensors
and Internet of Things (IoT) to leverage the power of big data, but they
are also innovative in how they engage citizens in co-creation and how
they leverage procurement dollars to improve city life. Perhaps most of
all, I believe smart cities are better able to attract, encourage, and harness
urban entrepreneurs.

In the past few years I have focused most of my academic research on
the emergence of different forms of entrepreneurship in urban environments and the roles cities play in fostering these innovators. I of course
have been inspired by those who have come before me, such as Richard
Florida, who graciously agreed to write the foreword to this book, and
revolutionary urbanists on both sides of the Atlantic such as Jane Jacobs
and Charles Landry. A few years ago I met Pablo Muñoz, who had just

Figure 0.1   Smart Cities Wheel

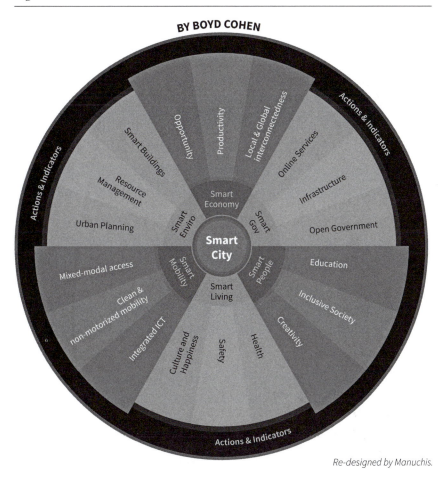

*Re-designed by Manuchis.*

finished his PhD in entrepreneurship at Newcastle University in the UK. Since then we have become great friends but also research colleagues with several projects related to the theme of this book. Many of the ideas in this book emerged from my work with Pablo, which is why I asked him to join me on this journey. I have also been working with Esteve Almirall, a research colleague, and Henry Chesbrough, the "father of open innovation" as guest editors for a special issue of the *California Management Review*, which focuses on the role of cities as a platform for open innovation and collaborative entrepreneurship.

By combining my practical experience as an entrepreneur in cities, with my academic research on sustainable innovation and smart cities,

I have developed a growing understanding of how cities are serving as breeding grounds for a range of urban entrepreneurs. I am incredibly optimistic about the future of innovation and entrepreneurship in urban environments, and this book seeks to share this optimism by exploring several key drivers for the boom in urban entrepreneurship, classifying types of urban entrepreneurs and exploring what cities, both large and small, are or should be doing to attract, retain, and harness their innovative potential. Since 2011, I have added a few more cities to my list of past homes: first Buenos Aires and later Santiago, Chile, where I wrote most of this book at the Universidad del Desarrollo, as the cofounder and academic director of the Center for Innovation in Cities. However, perhaps the story comes full circle for me, as I finished this book after moving to Barcelona, Spain. Barcelona has been calling me as both a scholar in the urban innovation arena and as a lover of walkable, vibrant, cosmopolitan, and inspiring cities. Barcelona is featured prominently here, but throughout the book I try to bring in unique and powerful stories of entrepreneurs, innovators, and cities that have inspired my thinking on urban entrepreneurship and innovation.

Finally, I wish to thank my wife, Elizabeth; my children, Mateo and Ayla; other family members, including Sharyn, Stuart, Judy, Bret, and Blair; and ABC-CLIO for believing in me and this project. I would also like to call out Pablo Muñoz, who was instrumental in providing critical, timely, and thorough advice on how to improve earlier drafts, which truthfully were far from ready for public viewing. The book you have in your hands or on your e-reader was greatly improved through Pablo's frequent written contributions and regular conversations with a local craft beer in our hands. Finally, I wish to thank the hundreds of people I have interviewed and met with over the course of the past few years who have contributed in their own way to this book. Many of them have been specifically cited throughout the chapters while many others have their voices and ideas reflected in the ideas on the pages in front of you.

# CHAPTER 1

## Emerging Urban Landscape for Innovation and Entrepreneurship

> People living in the first decade of the twentieth century did not know modern dental and medical equipment, penicillin, bypass operations, safe births, control of genetically transmitted diseases, personal computers, compact discs, television sets, automobiles, opportunities for fast and cheap worldwide travel, affordable universities, central heating, air conditioning ... technological change has transformed the quality of our lives.[1]

The innovation and entrepreneurship landscape of today is vastly different from even the tail end of the twentieth century. This chapter is dedicated to exploring three key driving forces—collaborative, democratized, and urbanized—that are changing the shape of innovation and entrepreneurship for the coming decades. This framework will help guide the discussion in the subsequent chapters on two distinctive forms of urbanpreneurship spaces: civic entrepreneurship and indie urbanpreneurship. These are the front-runners leading the urban entrepreneurship revolution.

### OUTDATED PARADIGMS OF INNOVATION AND ENTREPRENEURSHIP

After 100 years of industrial and technological revolutions, the past century demonstrated the global potential of the modern form of progress. Mass-produced cars of all types from companies around the globe, access to affordable air travel, and the proliferation of appliances in homes from microwaves to dishwashers all gained traction in industrial societies. We witnessed exponential growth in technological innovation from the introduction of the first massive mainframe computers to desktop computers, laptops, and smartphones. In 60 years, we moved from the Electronic Numerical Integrator and Computer, which required 30 tons to compute a flip-flop drive, to quantum computing, which no longer needs zeros and ones for a particular calculation, but physical particles (photons, electrons, etc.) that can be in all the states at the same time. In the past five decades, the world was introduced to the Internet, the resulting dot-com boom and bust and now the Internet of Things. Just to have an idea of this expansive growth, it is estimated that Internet speeds have increased by 50-fold in the last decade alone, driving our appetite for energy, leading some UK-based scientists, for example, to warn that this increment will end up using all of Britain's power supply by 2035.

For the most part, large multinational companies were behind these mass-produced innovations. In an era when CEOs like Andy Grove of Intel adopted the mantra "only the paranoid survive," companies competed on their capacity to internally develop innovative products on a continuous basis. This innovation capacity was seen as a core competitive advantage and a process that must be controlled and protected at all costs. Experts calculate that Apple, for example, spends an estimated $200 million a year fighting patent lawsuits against Android alone.[2] The *New York Times*, in 2012, citing research from Stanford University, noted:

as much as $20 billion was spent on patent litigation and patent purchases in the last two years—an amount equal to eight Mars rover missions. Last year, for the first time, spending by Apple and Google on patent lawsuits and unusually big-dollar patent purchases exceeded spending on research and development of new products, according to public filings.[3]

This is not to suggest that there was no place for new companies in the twentieth century. Out of Apple, Google, Cisco, and Facebook, only Apple was born before 1980 (1976), yet today they all occupy high-ranking positions in the Fortune 500. They were all born and raised, however, in the same era of paranoid CEOs and closed innovation. Apple, to this day, is one of the most secretive companies on the planet. And most of these tech pioneers, who emerged in the 1980s, were founded and grew in sprawling suburban tech parks, such as the glorified Silicon Valley, Boston's Route 128, and North Carolina's Research Triangle Park.

The tech boom of the latter twentieth century was largely financed by venture capitalists who take big risks in the hopes of big returns. In fact, the venture capital model generally assumes that only one of every 10 investments generates returns. But for the model to work, that one successful investment needs to return at least a 10× return on initial investment. A $10 million venture capital investment in a start-up, say in 1995, was hoped to generate a return of $100 million by 2000. This of course puts significant pressure on venture-backed start-up CEOs to scale their company fast and ideally find an exit within 5 years of venture financing. David Heinemeier Hansson, cofounder of Basecamp, an online project management tool, railed against the venture capital model in a 2015 blog post stating: "I wanted to put down roots. Long term bonds with coworkers and customers and the product. Impossible to steer and guide with a VC timebomb ticking that can only be defused by a 10–100× return."[4]

In 2012, the Kansas City–based Kauffman Foundation conducted a study of venture capital fund performance and the results were not pretty. Of 100 venture capital funds studied, only 20 generated better returns than average returns from public markets.[5] This is quite problematic because the majority of venture capitalists are not out to do good for the world; they are in it just for the money.

## THE EXPLOSION OF BUSINESS PLANS AND ENTREPRENEURSHIP COURSES IN BUSINESS SCHOOLS

In the age of venture capital and famous stories of 20 something college dropouts becoming billionaires overnight, university classrooms filled with people aspiring to become the next Michael Dell, Steve Jobs, or Mark Zuckerberg. In 1985, only 250 courses in the United States focused on entrepreneurship on annual basis, and by 2008, there were 5,000 entrepreneurship courses being taught at universities.[6] Results here are not that great either. Professor Pablo Martin de Holan reported in the *Financial Times* that only a quarter of an entrepreneurship-focused MBA graduating class end up starting a venture, and business schools are not revealing how many of these start-ups survive to see their thousandth day.[7] I suspect there are not so many. Having started my PhD in entrepreneurship at the University of Colorado in 1998, I can attest to the fact that back then, the overwhelming majority of entrepreneurship courses in the late twentieth century and early twenty-first century were focused on teaching students to form teams and develop a business plan for a new start-up idea. Most of these courses culminated in a presentation to potential venture capitalists and some even offered cash rewards and investment in the most promising start-ups. "Business schools are not serving entrepreneurs. They assume that learning how to build, tune and decorate a piano will automatically make you a good pianist," sarcastically insists Professor Pablo Martin de Holan.

It took me several years of teaching entrepreneurship, followed by my own forays into being an entrepreneur myself, to understand that not only was the venture capital model arguably broken, but so too was the approach to teaching entrepreneurship.

## TECHNOLOGY PUSH PARADIGM

If entrepreneurship is on the verge, even more so is technological innovation. In past decades, most companies, large and small, adopted the "build it they will come" philosophy of innovation. The prevailing concept was that companies knew what customers want. Customers were one-way recipients of what the market offered. Perhaps one of the best examples of this philosophy was embodied by the great debacle of Motorola's Iridium project. For younger readers, you might have to channel your parents to even consider the following scenario, but bear with me.

In the 1990s cellular communication was in its infancy. Cell phones were big, clunky, and frequently connected to passenger vehicles. Cell phones didn't roam well in those days. So you can imagine why a company like Motorola would recognize early that there could be a demand, especially for government officials, executives, and other frequent travelers, for a cell phone capable of roaming not just in the same city or within the same country but across borders. So Motorola executives and engineers began a very ambitious project to create the world's first global cell phone. Motorola spent 12 years building the business plan and the technology to support it. After launching 66 satellites into orbit to support the global cell phone coverage, Motorola began offering the phones and the service in 1998. Sounds great, right? Except for a few minor details. The phones cost about 3,000 (USD), weighed a few pounds, and usage fees were between $6 and $30 per minute! Probably not a shock to any readers too young to know this story, but the Iridium phones failed to gain any traction in the market. So, after spending more than $5 billion on the project, Iridium went into bankruptcy, giving Motorola the dubious distinction from *Time* magazine as one of the top 10 "Biggest Tech Failures of the Past Decade."[8] It was later saved by the Pentagon for use in remote battlefields but Motorola lost almost all of their investment and their mojo too. Turns out talking to customers before investing billions might actually be a smarter business strategy.

## PATENTS WERE SEEN AS PATHS TO PROFIT

Innovation can be expensive. Massive research and development (R&D) teams filled with engineers working on the next big thing. As the pace of innovation and competition increased throughout the past century, companies were keen to protect their investments and their innovations, which showed promise. Securing patents was a prerequisite to obtaining venture capital funding for most tech start-ups. Early patents emerged in the fifteenth century, but really started gaining prominence in the late 1900s and throughout the twentieth century. Initially, most patent systems were national in nature, but over time, the globalization of commerce and the complexity of seeking patents in every country a company wanted protection in became too cumbersome. The European Patent Office, initially consolidating patents for 16 European countries, came into being in 1977.

As innovation pioneer Carlota Perez emphasizes, technological revolutions are no longer about (paradoxically) technology. Accompanying the artifacts, there are codependent technoeconomic structures and behaviors, which play a role in rejuvenating the whole economy. Institutional, economic, and social changes host and receive the impacts of technological revolutions. Let's look at this more in detail.

## THE CHANGING ECONOMIC LANDSCAPE: NEW THINKING ON PURPOSE, PATENTS, AND PROFITS

We are at the cusp of some transformational sociotechnological changes that are already affecting our world in profound ways. We have witnessed major events that are shaping the future of our lives. Of course the "Great Recession" has had a long-lasting impact on the economy around the globe. It led to the Occupy Movement, which was driven by many who feel that the rich are getting richer and that there are declining opportunities for the middle class. Evidence suggests their concerns are rational. In the 1970s the top 1 percent of income earners in the United States represented 10 percent of total U.S. income, whereas by 2012 the top 1 percent earned 20 percent of the total U.S. income.[9] The developing world is even worse off. In Latin America, the poor represent 70 percent of the population, but obtain only 28 percent of total income. Market-wise, we are talking about 406 million people who spend $760 billion every year on basic goods and services, but still struggle frequently earning less than $10 a day. Unhappiness with the perception of growing income disparities and austerity measures implemented in several countries have even led to new political parties. In Spain, the Podemos ("We Can") party was born as a result of the Occupy Movement in the country. A center-right party in Spain also emerged, which is called Ciudadanos ("Citizens"), whose base is primarily young and urban and whose focus for addressing income disparity and unemployment is by concentrating on growing the innovation economy in cities throughout the country.

Furthermore the amount of citizen watchdogs and public shaming of corporations acting exclusively for profit maximization at the expense of doing what is right has caused the corporate world and business schools to rethink the profit maximization paradigm. Take the recent case of Volkswagen and their defrauding the global public on the pollutants created by their diesel, TDI, vehicles. Volkswagen and the German auto industry, in general, has been seen as a pillar of efficiency, environmental leadership, and innovation. Yet, Volkswagen engineers were either unable or unwilling to find a technical solution to reduce the pollutants from their diesel engines and instead decided to invent a clever, but shockingly unethical and deceitful, software solution that modified the TDI vehicles' driving behavior only when the cars were being tested for pollutants. In just two days following the revelations that millions of vehicles in the United States and around the world were altered, Volkswagen's stock fell 35 percent resulting in shareholder losses of 25 billion euros.[10] Credit Suisse has estimated the eventual losses for Volkswagen due to the scandal could reach 78 billion euros![11] Not only did billions go out the door, as well as their CEO, Martin Winterkorn, but perhaps even more importantly, so too did the consumer confidence and brand loyalty Volkswagen had built over many decades.

## THE EMERGENCE OF THE PURPOSE ECONOMY

While business schools and most corporations have focused on profit maximization, we are now witnessing a transition to the "purpose economy." In 2001, as I was finishing my PhD, I was handed the book *Natural Capitalism*, published in 1999 by Paul Hawken, Amory B. Lovins, and L. Hunter Lovins. This book was a global best seller and helped to usher in a new way of thinking about the relationship between industry, society, and the natural environment. Following *The Next Economy* and *The Ecology of Commerce*, *Natural Capitalism* presented a compelling case for how companies could embrace social and environmental responsibility and actually be even more profitable. I was inspired to pursue academic research and later my own green start-ups, in large part due to the insights I gleaned from *Natural Capitalism*. This led me to coauthor the sequel to *Natural Capitalism*, called *Climate Capitalism*, in 2011 with L. Hunter Lovins to demonstrate the business case for the low-carbon economy.

We have already seen a great amount of pioneering innovation and thought-leadership with regard to economic activity with greater purpose. In 2014, Aaron Hurst published the *Purpose Economy* to demonstrate the shift ongoing from traditional consumerism and profit maximization toward a more inclusive approach to business and economic activity.

Perhaps one of the clearest examples of this has been the emergence of new corporate forms and the Certified B-Corporation movement, which counts more than 1,300 members in 41 countries. The B-Corporation website explains that "B Corps are certified by the nonprofit B Lab to meet rigorous standards of social and environmental performance, accountability, and transparency." What makes B Corps unique is that they incorporate into their charter a formal obligation to adhere to rigorous social and environmental standards, which means that their shareholders are the only stakeholder B Corps are accountable to. Whereas those of us trained in business schools under Harvard Business School's famed Michael Porter's competitive mantra were encouraged to consider the primary, if not exclusive, responsibility of firms is to maximize shareholder wealth, business school students today are actually learning about sustainable and social entrepreneurship, B Corporations, and Porter's Shared Value framework. According to Mike Stoddard of the Association of MBAs (AMBA), which represents more than 200 business schools around the globe:

In research carried out by AMBA over the last few years, students, alumni and employers highlighted the value of sustainability, and its increasing importance over time. Almost 80% of business schools agreed that sustainability is an important part of the MBA curriculum.[12]

Some schools have even adopted sustainability as the central motto, such as Vermont's Sustainable Entrepreneurship MBA, Exeter's One Planet MBA, Bainbridge Graduate Institute, and Leeds's Sustainability and Business Masters of Science.

Aside from the aforementioned changes shaping our economic environment, I have identified three factors that are converging to change innovation and entrepreneurship in a decidedly urban fashion. These include the emergence of the sharing economy and collaborative business models, democratization of innovation and urbanization, which combine to form what I refer to as the Urbanpreneur Spiral.

## THE URBANPRENEUR SPIRAL

We're in ground zero for Silicon Valley and we're doing more innovations than in the past. We're now looking at cities without taxis with Uber, cities without hotels, bikes we never had before and new forms of entrepreneurship in the digital age with Google and Lyft. There's a whole new way for the millennial dweller that we're exploring.[13]

—Tom Cochran, CEO of the U.S. Conference of Mayors

I have been researching, teaching, and participating in the innovation and entrepreneurship arena for nearly two decades. In fact, the first ever study I completed, with colleagues at the University of Colorado, Boulder, involved interviews with dozens of entrepreneurs and others participating in the local entrepreneurial ecosystem in an attempt to understand what factors influence the vibrancy of a local entrepreneurial ecosystem. At that time we were not thinking so much about the city of Boulder but rather the region including the growth of the tech community in a suburban tech park, Colorado Technology Center, based in Louisville, Colorado. In our early research, similar to the recent work of Brad Feld, which incidentally was largely drawn from insights he has gathered working in the Boulder area entrepreneurial ecosystem, we were focused on high-growth, technology-based, venture capital–backed, start-up communities, which historically were based in suburban tech parks.

Based on my own research and entrepreneurial activity, and that of others I respect, I now believe that the majority of innovation and entrepreneurship will no longer occur in the suburbs, that it will be less dependent on venture capital than it used to be, and that it will increasingly result from new approaches to collaborative business models and the sharing economy. From these insights I have developed the Urbanpreneur Spiral to reflect the collaborative, urbanized, and democratized nature of emerging innovation and entrepreneurship ecosystems (Figure 1.1).

### Urbanized

The United Nations has documented that in 2008, for the first time in human history, more than half of the world's population was living in cities. Estimates suggest that by 2050, that ratio will climb to 67 percent, with 1.3 million people moving to cities each week.[14] There are many reasons for the massive urban migration, mostly the perceived improved quality of life and access to economic opportunities in cities. Cities are increasingly driving the global economy as well. In 2011, the global

Figure 1.1   The Urbanpreneur Spiral

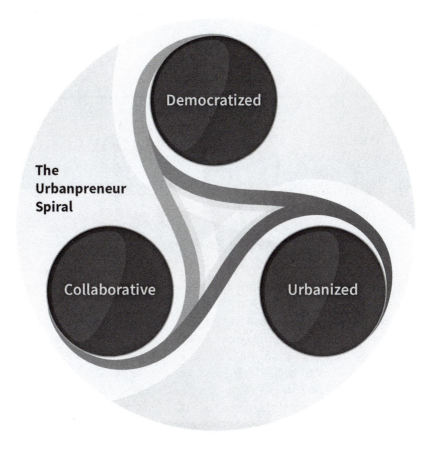

strategy consultancy McKinsey sought out to understand how the largest cities in the world are shaping the global economy. Some of their results were surprising. They identified 600 of the largest cities in the world (Global 600) and determined that those 600 cities represent 22 percent of the world's population and 60 percent of global GDP. Perhaps even more surprising was the study's prediction that by 2025, 136 new cities will enter the Global 600 and 100 of them will be from China! Even more awe inspiring is the fact that the Chinese government is currently working on integrating Beijing with Tianjin and Hebei to develop an urban area with 130 million people. The sustainable city rattles my brain when I visualize a third of the United States living in an area the size of Idaho.

Thus, the world is urbanizing and so too is the economy, against the predictions of suburban, pro-agglomeration economists. Furthermore, drivers of economic growth, innovation and entrepreneurship, are naturally urbanizing as well.

Of course Richard Florida, who graciously wrote the foreword to this book, was among the first to recognize this trend and to explore how the creative class are seeking higher quality of life in culturally diverse and vibrant cities. Florida has begun to demonstrate a major shift in preferences for tech start-ups that no longer wish to be confined to monolithic suburban sprawled tech parks and prefer to be closer to the center of cities.

Other researchers have also been tracking the demographics of urbanization. For example, the City Observatory published a report that 37 percent more college-educated young adults between the ages of 25 and 34 were living in city centers in the United States in 2013 than in 2000.[15]

This contributes to the next factor of the Urbanpreneur Spiral, the democratization of innovation and technology.

## Democratization of Innovation and Technology

By and large, the major tech companies that emerged in the twentieth century were founded by a relatively elite set of entrepreneurs, frequently having attended (although not always graduated from) prestigious universities, possessed strong personal networks, and either lived in or migrated to the major suburban tech parks in the United States or around the globe. This "old boys club"—and boys is appropriate since less than 10 percent of venture-backed start-ups have female founders[16]—is gradually giving way to a distributed set of nodes of innovation and entrepreneurship in cities around the globe. In 2005, Eric von Hippel published the seminal book *Democratizing Innovation*, which suggested that increasingly users are engaging more in the innovation process and that in the future, innovation would be much more bottom-up rather than top-down. Von Hippel's model was consistent with the introduction of *Open Innovation* by Henry Chesbrough of the University of California Berkeley. *Open Innovation*, much like von Hippel's work, was initially focused on how corporations are engaging users in the innovation process. However, the concepts of democratized and open innovation have expanded significantly since then and go well beyond bringing users into corporate innovation programs. They are also related to the rapidly declining costs of technology and innovation tools, making them more accessible to larger populations beyond the good old boys' network of venture capital–backed start-ups. Below I will address three driving features of democratized innovation and technology in modern times: (1) open innovation, (2) declining costs combined with increased access to innovation and technology tools and crowdfunding, and (3) the subsequent decline in dependence on venture capital.

### Democratized: From Closed Innovation to Open Innovation

Earlier I discussed the epic failure of Motorola's Iridium project. That very costly and embarrassing disaster could have been avoided had Microsoft embraced user-centric, design-driven innovation processes. Today, numerous universities are offering programs built around design thinking, encouraging students and executives to embrace the development of empathy for the user. Even Harvard's MBA is slowly moving away from the ruthless competitive strategy toward promoting empathy as part of the company business model. Rather than "build it they will come," today's innovators are co-creating solutions with users in mind from the beginning. In the world of entrepreneurship, this approach has been widely embraced via the introduction of new approaches such as the Lean Start-up methodology. Lean Start-up methodology, made popular by Eric Ries and adapted to the university education context by Steve Blank, compels entrepreneurs to eschew massive business plans and 5-year financial spreadsheets complete with hockey stick growth projections. Instead, Lean Start-up adherents are encouraged to build a one-page business model canvas and to introduce an iterative, user-based set of trial and error via a minimum viable product (MVP). The idea behind MVPs is rather than spending billions on sending satellites into orbit and designing a 5-pound phone that works only outdoors, it is more prudent to quickly introduce a massively scaled-down, even virtual or on-paper, version of the planned product to gain early and regular feedback on the concept from potential users. As a result, the new process involves both customer and product development.

Note that the Lean Start-up is not about taking surveys of what future customers might be willing to pay for a product in the future. Rather it is about getting early feedback from users interacting with a mockup or base prototype before building the product. My best friend from my doctoral program at the University of Colorado, Heidi Neck, who is now a senior faculty member at Babson College and one of the foremost experts on entrepreneurship education, summed up to me succinctly her opinion on business plans in the early stages of venture formation: "Writing a business plan too early is simply an excuse not to take action." Heidi's opinion is backed up by the shift from business plan competitions at Babson College and MIT toward a focus more on judging student startups on their MVP. Even the U.S. Association for Small Business and

Entrepreneurship (USASBE) changed their annual competition from business planning to the creation of testable business models and early customer traction.

Even Apple, who historically has been one of the most secretive companies on the planet, has started to embrace open innovation. Open innovation, first coined by Henry Chesbrough in his 2003 best-selling book, is an approach to innovation that embraces the distributed nature of good ideas. Rather than rely exclusively on internal innovation capacity, companies embracing open innovation turn to customers, suppliers, and other stakeholders to help generate ideas and occasionally even co-produce new products and services. Apple's App Store is a great example of open innovation in that Apple provides the platform, software, and the installed (and continuously growing) user base of iPhones and allows third party developers to come up with their own innovative ideas for how to add value to iPhone users. I am not going to argue that all 2 million apps available for the iPhone should qualify as innovative or that Apple is completely open to open innovation. Yet the App Store has also proven to support a range of productive and less-productive but widely used apps. In 2014, third party app developers for the iPhone earned $10 billion in revenues from app sales and in-app purchases. Lest you think Apple is allowing this open innovation ecosystem in a gesture of altruism, think again. Apple gained $4.5 billion in revenue in 2014 alone from their share of the revenue earned by being a platform between developers and iPhone users.[17]

### *Democratized: The Decline of Patents?*

Recall the historical focus on protecting innovation with patents? I do not expect the future to be void of patents and closed innovation. There will still be valid reasons to protect company secrets and secure patents. But we are already witnessing an important shift toward open innovation and sharing intellectual property. Despite being an early player in the hybrid vehicle market, Toyota has spent several years working on fuel cell–powered vehicles. In 2016, Toyota released the first production-scale fuel cell vehicle (FCV) called the Mirai. Toyota realizes this technology has an uphill climb because of the barriers for safely making, storing, and distributing hybrid fuel compared with the growing interest in electric vehicles. In the process of developing its fuel cell vehicle, Toyota sought and obtained patent protection for a range of innovations required to bring the Mirai to market. In total, Toyota obtained 5,680 patents pertaining to its FCV development. In January 2015, Toyota announced it was releasing all of its patents to the market, including its competitors, in hopes of accelerating the development of more FCVs and obviously growing the fuel cell production and distribution marketplace. So much for "only the paranoid survive."

Toyota is not the only nor was it the first automobile manufacturer to embrace the idea of opening up their patents to their competitors. Elon Musk, Tesla's dynamic CEO, announced on June 12, 2014, that the company would release all of its patents, embracing the open source movement in the software industry. I will let Musk speak for himself regarding the motivation for the apparently drastic move, one unheard of just a few years ago.

Yesterday, there was a wall of Tesla patents in the lobby of our Palo Alto headquarters. That is no longer the case. They have been removed, in the spirit of the open source movement, for the advancement of electric vehicle technology.

Tesla Motors was created to accelerate the advent of sustainable transport. If we clear a path to the creation of compelling electric vehicles, but then lay intellectual property landmines behind us to inhibit others, we are acting in a manner contrary to that goal. Tesla will not initiate patent lawsuits against anyone who, in good faith, wants to use our technology.

When I started out with my first company, Zip2, I thought patents were a good thing and worked hard to obtain them. ... After Zip2, when I realized that receiving a patent really just meant that you bought a lottery ticket to a lawsuit, I avoided them whenever possible. ... We believe that applying the open source philosophy to our patents will strengthen rather than diminish Tesla's position in this regard.[18]

The Toyota and Tesla examples suggest that today, patents are perhaps less important than they were previously, and that by embracing the democratization of innovation, firm performance may actually be enhanced more than by keeping innovation in-house.

Another major challenge to patents: patent systems do not encourage innovation and have often been found to have the reverse effect of stifling innovation. In recently published research reviewing prior research and patent and innovation information since the 1800s, Petra Moser, a Stanford University professor of economics, concluded:

Historical evidence suggests that in countries with patent laws, the majority of innovations occur outside of the patent system. Countries without patent laws have produced as many innovations as countries with patent laws during some time periods, and their innovations have been of comparable quality. Even in countries with relatively modern patent laws, such as the mid-nineteenth-century United States, most inventors avoided patents and relied on alternative mechanisms when these were feasible.[19]

### Democratized: The Declining Costs for Urbanpreneurs

It is just plain cheaper to build many companies today than it used to be. We now have cloud computing eliminating the need for onsite servers. Early-stage companies can leverage on-demand economy solutions like Elance to build cheap prototypes offshore, open source software is much more plentiful, and the growth of incubators, accelerators, and coworking spaces has decreased the need for expensive office space. Internet access is ubiquitous in most developed countries (and many developing ones too) including free public Wi-Fi hotspots in airports and throughout dense (and lately not so dense) municipal areas. The global number of public hotspots has grown exponentially in five years (2009–2014), from 500 thousand to 4.5 million, and nearly 6 million by the end of 2015. The number for private hotspots is equally impressive. From 233 to 646 million in the 2009–2015 period.[20] Facebook even recently initiated a project designed to bring satellite-based Internet access to the African continent, frequently free of charge. Furthermore, the growing distribution of broadband networks to homes and communities around the globe also contributes to democratization. The U.S. Federal Communications Commission (FCC) Commissioner Ajit Pai recently noted, "Broadband has a democratizing effect on society most notably in entrepreneurship."[21]

An article by Austin Smith in *Venture Beat* sums up the declining costs of starting up companies in what they refer to as the era of Entrepreneurship 3.0 quite well:

Beginning in the early 2000s, instead of selling your car to afford hardware, you could sell a coffee table and afford it. Over the past 15 years, many costs associated with building products—servers, databases, all the once-homerolled things that are now available as cheap SaaS products—dropped immensely.

This ushered in an era where startups were lean and could do with $250,000 what a startup in the '90s could do with $2,500,000. It led to 10 times more products launching, 10 times as fast. It's been a prosperous and successful era for the Internet. Only a few costs remained high: labor, office space, accounting, legal, marketing, etc ... it dawned on me that we're now entering a new era, and all those remaining costs—labor, office space, accounting, legal, marketing, etc.—are dropping to the floor. Just like last time around, it's going to mean that we see 10 times more products launching, 10 times as fast. It means we can do with $250 what a startup five years ago could do with $250,000.[22]

Beyond the declining costs for traditional start-ups, there are now new resources for makers such as 3D labs and Fabrication Labs (i.e., Fab Labs).

In fact Fab Labs, by requirement, must be free to use for residents of the local community. These resources, combined with new online platforms for connecting to potential consumers around the globe like Etsy, can turn people normally considered hobbyists into indie urbanpreneurs, the subject of Chapter 4.

If entrepreneurs no longer need the massive space found in suburban tech parks to house expensive servers, and if entrepreneurs can increasingly get by in the early stages with fewer employees, they can also increasingly use the growing amount of incubator and co-working spaces that are popping up in cities around the globe. As such, many urbanpreneurs are turning to crowdfunding instead of traditional angel investors or venture capital.

### Democratized: Declining Role of Venture Capital and Increased role of Crowdfunding

Most entrepreneurship thought leaders and scholars, in my opinion, place too much importance on the role of capital. In 2014, Up Global for example developed a white paper analyzing the success factors of entrepreneurial ecosystems and found five key ingredients: talent, start-up density, culture, capital, and regulatory environment.[23] Similarly, in Brad Feld's important book on this topic, *Startup Communities*, he too reinforced the critical role a vibrant venture capital community has on local entrepreneurial ecosystems. Of course, this is natural given his background as a venture capitalist.

While it is hard to disagree with this logic, my research and observations of innovation and entrepreneurship activity in cities suggests that venture capital is nice to have but not as critical as it used to be, at least in the early stages of new venture development.

Aside from the declining costs of innovation and entrepreneurship, inventors and entrepreneurs are increasingly turning to crowdfunding as an alternative source of early stage financing as opposed to equity-based angel and venture capital funding. Crowdfunding comes from virtual platforms allowing aspiring entrepreneurs to easily tap into national and even global consumers to pre-purchase their innovations. Crowdfunding has become big business. There are more than 700 different crowdfunding platforms online. Between 2009 and 2012 the global funding volume of crowdfunding platforms increased from 530 to 2,800 million (USD). In 2015 the number was estimated to reach 34 billion (USD) and the World Bank projected global crowdfunding to near 100 billion (USD) by 2025.[24] It is not difficult to forecast that crowdfunding and other alternative forms of investment will continue their expansion as the formal financial system continues to prove its tendency to crash.

This does not mean that venture capital is going to disappear. Even successful crowdfunded companies will continue to seek venture capital if they intend to scale the venture on a national or global level. This of course will create a new dynamic between entrepreneur and venture capitalist since one of the biggest challenges for early-stage entrepreneurs is the perceived risk that there is insufficient market demand for their new products. Power imbalances and information asymmetries between entrepreneurs and funders will most likely move to a new ground. I guess we will need to revisit the traditional "Dragons' Den" image where entrepreneurs beg for financial help. Successful crowdfunding campaigns help reduce the risk by providing an important form of early market validation. I would be surprised if we do not see the emergence of new forms of venture capital, geared toward successful crowdfunded start-ups whereby the formula for calculating valuations and equity ownership for venture capitalists is significantly revised, in favor of the crowdfunded start-up.

San Diego–based Ryan Gepper provides a unique and fascinating insight into this modern approach to preselling yet-to-be-manufactured products via crowdfunding while, at least temporarily, avoiding equity dilution from venture capitalists. Gepper quit his job in the medical field more than a decade ago to become a full-time inventor. After several failed inventions, Gepper felt it was time to bring beverage coolers into the twenty-first century. He developed an early prototype of a high-tech cooler concept and launched a Kickstarter campaign toward the end of 2013. He didn't meet his $125,000 goal so the campaign failed. He took the lessons learned, advanced his MVP, and launched a new campaign. Originally seeking just $50,000 for this second campaign, he actually generated more than $13 million mostly in presales.

Crowdfunding is certainly changing the dynamic between start-ups and the venture capital community. Take Pebble's experience as an example. Eric Migicovsky, founder of Pebble smart watch, gained acceptance into the famous Y Combinator accelerator and shortly after raised $375,000 in angel funding. Yet, more than 20 venture capitalists were unwilling to invest the money required to manufacture the smart watch at scale. Commenting on their inability to raise venture capital investment, Migicovsky stated:

I wasn't extremely surprised . . . hardware is much harder to raise money for. We were hoping we could convince some people to our vision, but it didn't work out.[25]

So the founders turned to Kickstarter, in what turned out to be one of the most successful crowdfunding campaigns in history. Migicovsky launched the Kickstarter campaign on April 11, 2012, hoping to obtain $100,000 in commitments, primarily to presell a smart watch that was in development at the time. After only two days of the campaign, the two-man Pebble team had already reached their campaign target. On May 18, 2012, the campaign was closed after raising more than $10 million from nearly 69,000 backers in just over 1 month. The Pebble team also enabled the donation offer, which appealed to 2615 backers. The remaining backers pre-purchased Pebble's smart watch in volumes Migicovsky could have never imagined.

The success of Pebble's Kickstarter campaign did not go unnoticed as Pebble was able to raise a $15 million Series A round led by Charles River Ventures in May, 2013, about 1 year to the day after their crowdfunding campaign closed. The use of funds from the Series A was targeted toward engineering team expansion and increased production capability to meet the demand generated by the Kickstarter campaign. At the launch of the Kickstarter campaign, Pebble had two full-time staff, including Eric. By March 2014, Pebble had 70 employees. Between January 2013 and March 2014 Pebble had sold 400,000 watches and in 2015 they had more than doubled that number to 1 million.[26]

The influence of crowdfunding is true not only for tech start-ups. In 2012, Oakland-based Back to the Roots secured a 250,000 (USD) investment from 2,800 backers in just a few weeks to develop the final prototype of a simple, yet innovative self-cleaning fish tank that also grows food. This is remarkable because they needed only 100,000 USD to develop the Home Aquaponics Kit.

Crowdfunding is leveling the playing field in many ways. For example, a recent study of crowdfunding projects on Kickstarter found that 69.5 percent of women were successful in achieving their campaign goals compared with 61.4 percent of male-founded campaigns.[27] Another interesting factor, leading even further to the distributed nature of innovation and entrepreneurship, is that the mean distance between a crowdfunding investor or customer is 3,000 miles while the average distance between a venture capital fund's headquarters and their investees is only 70 miles![28] Thus, crowdfunding may have an equalizing effect, not only removing the dependence of entrepreneurs to be located near lots of venture capitalists but also breaking down gender and hopefully racial and other discriminatory barriers erected by the old boys' club.

The democratization of innovation and technology through open innovation, declining costs of technology tools, and crowdfunding are all

changing the landscape of innovation and entrepreneurship and are contributing to the growth of urbanpreneurship in cities throughout the
globe. The last factor in the Urbanpreneur Spiral is collaborative, which
has clear links to the open innovation and crowdsourced insights
discussed above.

## COLLABORATIVE

Open innovation originated from the idea of corporations embracing
users in the innovation process. However, as open innovation expanded,
first within corporations and later to other sectors including start-ups and
even cities themselves, the importance of collaboration as a driver in
innovation processes became even more apparent. Open and collaborative innovation are not actually the same. Instead of just engaging potential users regarding desirable features of products, companies began to
open up more of their innovation activities with users and even with
competitors. The opening up of patent portfolios of Toyota and Tesla
are two such examples of the latter. Yet today, companies, start-ups, and
cities are increasing the degree of collaboration with users/citizens in
the hopes of co-creating new solutions. Crowdsourcing, for example,
can be a way for organizations to solicit not just ideas to improve existing
or planned product rollouts, but also to introduce new products. In some
instances users or makers actually create prototypes, virtually with 3D
modeling or even physical products with 3D printers.

The collaborative factor of the Urbanpreneur Spiral is primarily com-
posed of two drivers: the increased interest in collaborative business models and the growth of the collaborative (or sharing) economy.

### Collaborate: Collaborative Business Models

Trends suggest today's innovators are ushering in an increased presence
of collaborative business models where multiple firms, citizens, and even
governments are baking in collaboration into the DNA from the outset
of the enterprise. The global consultancy Accenture refers to this next
generation collaboration as a "virtual vertical mindset" whereby instead
of the traditional supplier-retailer arm's-length relationship, they present
a set of concentric circles to illustrate that collaboration requires much
more integration between partners and collaborators to be able to innovate faster and keep up with the rapidly growing set of online competitors
who are often able to dis-intermediate the traditional retail value chain.
But the growth in collaborative business models goes well beyond

traditional retailers. The continued growth of collaborative technology tools from video conferencing to open source online project management tools facilitates even more local and global collaboration among various stakeholders.

The new technologies, collaborative business models, and organizational forms supported by networking tools "invade" all traditional businesses and organizations which requires thinking in terms of whole systems, i.e. seeing each business as part of a wider economic ecosystem and environment.[29]

Yet the increasing role of collaboration goes beyond traditional B2B connections and can emerge outside the Western market artifact. In the early 2000s, C. K. Prahalad and Stuart Hart introduced the concept of the base or bottom of the pyramid, referring to the potential for economic opportunities and impact for multinationals seeking to gain access to the rapidly growing markets in the developing world. Increasingly companies have embraced the idea of reaching the base of the pyramid through collaborations with multinational and local NGOs.

The advocacy, operations and service delivery of many NGOs is designed to ameliorate intractable social and environmental problems, working on multiple issues including combating hunger, curtailing human rights abuses, countering environmental degradation and improving health care. NGOs and for-profit corporations are also developing more collaborative relationships of potential mutual benefit. Their relationships with NGOs can provide corporations with access to different resources, competencies and capabilities than are otherwise available internally, or which they might acquire from alliances with other for-profit organizations.[30]

In recent years, new business models from purpose-based enterprises have sought to bake in base of the pyramid impact through collaborations with consumers and NGOs in local markets in the developing world. Tom's Shoes founder, Blake Mycoskie, is from Arlington, Texas, and founded his company in Santa Monica, California. Yet, Mycoskie's mission has been to create social impact by encouraging customers in the developed world to purchase Tom's shoes with each purchased pair being matched with a free pair delivered to children in the developing world. The shoes are delivered through partnerships with local organizations on the ground in their target impact communities. Arguably the most transformative collaborative models emerging today are those associated with the collaborative economy, sometimes referred to as the sharing economy.

### Collaborative: From Ownership to Access

In the past few years we have seen an explosion in "collaborative economy" start-ups. As Rachel Botsman articulated convincingly in her 2010 book *What's Mine Is Yours*, the sharing economy promises to transform industry, communities, and quality of life by shifting our collective consumer patterns away from ownership of goods and services toward on-demand access of goods and services. That circular saw you bought three years ago to install hardwood flooring in your living room. Are you sure you need to keep that in your garage collecting dust for eternity until it no longer works and you need to dispose of it? The idea of the sharing, or collaborative, economy is to find ways to optimize underutilized resources in ways that can lead to a win-win between the owner and the user, and the environment too. I feel a little embarrassed to admit that I have owned a drill for years and used it only for a few minutes, which is not a surprise when the average power drill is used for somewhere between 6 and 20 minutes in its entire lifetime.[31]

The actual definition of sharing economy and what falls in or out of it is still under dispute, as in any pre-paradigmatic field. Yet, sharing constitutes an unavoidable reality that we need to address, even under a cloud of contestations.

### Sharing Platforms

Sharing economy start-ups that have generated the most press to date have utilized platform business models. Much like Apple's App Store, these platforms serve as an intermediary to connect developers/owners and buyers/users seeking access. Launched in Amsterdam, a leading player in Europe's sharing cities space, Peerby.com enables people in the same community to share underutilized resources such as drills, trailers, party equipment, tents, and garden scissors for free among each other. Having participated in accelerators like Techstars and a few million in venture capital investment, Peerby is now active in dozens of cities in Europe and the U.S.

Airbnb, the current poster child for scalable sharing economy platforms, connects owners of excess housing capacity to people seeking temporary housing from a day to months. Airbnb offers more than 1 million listings from couches in someone's apartment to entire castles (over 600 of them). Despite not owning a single hotel or bedroom, Airbnb is on pace to rent out more rooms per night than the largest hotel chains in the world by 2016. Furthermore, in 2015, Airbnb had a valuation of 24 billion (USD) and projected revenues of 900 million (USD), making it larger than Marriott and ranking it as one of the largest hospitality companies in the world.[32] Not bad for a company founded in 2008 that serves only as a platform and has no tangible capital investment in real estate.

Of course, many collaborative economy companies have faced legal challenges from cities and from incumbent industries. The behemoth sharing economy players, mostly founded in Silicon Valley, have developed a less-than-stellar reputation in cities around the globe. In fact, these players seeking global market domination have been referred to as "platform death stars" by the leading advocate for responsible sharing economy, Shareable.net. Of course, part of the angst with the "death stars" is that they have embraced the Silicon Valley, venture-capital motto of world domination. Earlier in this chapter I quoted the founder of Bascamp, who criticized the venture capital scaling requirements as inconsistent with building long-term relationships. Hansson suggested that the venture capital–inspired goals for startups to dominate their industry segment can be poisonous to anyone who gets in their way, including communities. This is the same concern echoed by Shareable's founder, Neal Gorenflo:

Uber signifies a new era in tech entrepreneurship. Its leaders express an explicit ideology of domination and limitless, global ambition. In fact, the global tech sector may be one of the most powerful stateless actors on the world stage today. And Death Star platforms are the tech sector's avant garde.

Death Star platforms deftly exploit today's growing economic insecurity and political vacuum. Their business model relies on precarious 1099 contractors. They mix technology, ideology, design, public relations, community organizing, and lobbying in a powerful new formulation that's conquering cities and users around the world. They wrap themselves in the cloak of technological progress, free market inevitability, and even common good. As a result, cities allow them to break their laws with surprising frequency (Uber and Airbnb are simply illegal in most cities). Weak city governments either drink the Kool-Aid or struggle to contain them.[33]

In 2013 I was invited to do a keynote speech on the intersection of smart cities and tourism for the Vienna Tourism Board. Naturally I brought up the increasing importance of the sharing economy in cities and showed the number of Airbnb listings available to me during my visit. Not surprisingly, some members of the Tourism Board stated that this was a very controversial topic as the city is losing tax revenue and the hotel industry was facing the additional competition brought by Airbnb listings in their city. My response was that Airbnb and other sharing economy platform providers are likely here to stay and that cities, and especially tourism boards, need to become more proactive in collaborating with and regulating the collaborative economy so that ideally there is a win-win for everyone through increased tourism revenue making the city accessible to a wider target audience. Besides, as the recently appointed head of global policy at Airbnb stresses, sharing platforms not only give access to underutilized resources but also help in tackling pressing problems such as income inequality and climate change, unavoidable issues for mayors across the world. While it makes sense to fight taxation problems in the short term, mayors and tourism boards alike should be reflecting on how to use the sharing economy and the entrepreneurs behind it to benefit their cities.

The role of cities in supporting or discouraging this emergent space will be discussed in Chapters 5 and 6. However, one place to turn for insights on where collaborative economy players and cities may end up is the Airbnb project in Portland. In 2014, Brian Chesky, co-founder of Airbnb, launched a pilot program in Portland called Shared City. In Chesky's own words:

Imagine if you could build a city that is shared. Where people become micro-entrepreneurs, and local mom and pops flourish once again. Imagine a city that fosters community, where space isn't wasted, but shared with others. A city produces more, but without more waste. While this may seem radical, it's not a new idea. Cities are the original sharing platforms. They formed at ancient crossroads of trade, and grew through collaboration and sharing resources. But over time, they began to feel mass produced. We lived closer together, but drifted further apart. But sharing in cities is back, and we want to help build this future. We are committed to helping make cities stronger socially, economically and environmentally. We are committed to enriching the neighborhoods we serve. . . .

To honor these commitments, and to realize a more enriched city, today we are announcing Shared City . . . (In partnership with the Mayor) . . . We're offering to cut red tape and to collect and remit taxes to the city of Portland on behalf of our hosts. This is new for us, and if it works well for our community and cities, we may replicate this project in other U.S. cities.[34]

I realize that sounds a lot more like hyperbole than a CEO necessarily committed to collaborating with cities. Certainly Airbnb has a vested interest in overcoming city barriers to their business model and Shared City is one way to do that. Aside from the Shared City initiative, Airbnb has committed to serving communities in times of disaster. After Hurricane Sandy in New York City in 2012, Airbnb facilitated the use of its platform and properties for free via 1,400 listers in New York City who agreed to make their homes available to those displaced from the storm. Victoria, Australia, entered into an agreement with Airbnb to help facilitate a similar approach in the event of future disasters. I would hardly argue that Airbnb is an altruistic, purpose-based sharing economy platform, yet they are pioneering new forms of collaboration with local governments in hopes of achieving synergistic benefits with the cities where they operate, the Airbnb community of renters and urbanpreneurs, and of course, Airbnb shareholders.

Uber not unlike Airbnb has been under attack because of their surge pricing during chaotic times and because of Uber's avoidance of traditional taxi regulations. In fact, many observers of the sharing economy would argue that Uber is actually not a participant of the sharing economy in the sense that it is not really a platform for peer-to-peer collaborations but rather a largely unregulated private taxi fleet.

The collaborative economy has the potential to become a transformative paradigm by supporting a shift in global and local cultures from ownership toward access. One need look no further than their closet to identify underutilized resources. Remember that dress you wore once to your best friend's wedding and has been untouched for two years? There are platforms for sharing these items with others in need of them where you receive some compensation in return for letting a vetted stranger borrow it for a few days. Sounds like a small idea? Rent the Runway, founded in 2009 by two Harvard Business School students, Jenn Hyman and Jenny Fleiss, the largest platform for clothes sharing or renting, was recently valued at $600 million in its latest funding round.[35]

What works for clothing and hospitality also works for hand tools, paintings, furniture, allotment gardens, cars, leftovers, and much more. I guess dental floss might be out of the sharing equation but most things we own are underutilized and could be shared.

In a study completed in 2015 by the global consultancy Price Waterhouse Coopers (PwC) involving a poll of 1,000 adults in the United States, 60 percent of respondents agreed that access is the new

ownership and 72 percent of the respondents expected to be active participants in the collaborative economy within the next two years.[36]

Jeremiah Owyang, founder of Crowd Companies, and arguably the
most recognized thought leader in the collaborative economy arena,
has been documenting the companies, trends, and opportunities shaping the sharing economy marketplace. Owyang has identified thousands of companies participating in the sharing economy across a
dozen categories such as money (crowdfunding), space, transportation,
services, goods, food, logistics, and more. According to Owyang,
between 2010 and 2015, sharing economy start-ups had raised
more than $11 billion from investors.[37] Remember, I didn't say that
venture capital was dead, just that it is not the only way start-ups can
raise money these days.

The collaborative economy is growing rapidly and destined for big
things, including big opportunities for start-ups. These start-ups, and the
opportunities they are capitalizing on, are predominately occurring in
cities. As Pablo and I wrote in a recent publication on sharing cities:

While not exclusive to cities, the sharing economy is gaining more traction in
urban areas because they are where dense populations and ICTs such as smart
phones and high speed internet coexist. We suggest that cities are also faced with
scarce resources and insufficient infrastructure capacity which require innovations in consumption and production systems to maintain or improve quality of
life for all.[38]

Thus, not only might the sharing economy present significant opportunities for entrepreneurs, while reducing the collective environmental footprint of cities, but it also has the potential to increase access for lower
income people who would otherwise not be able to afford the possessions
they can now share. These points have led some cities such as Seoul,
South Korea, and Amsterdam, The Netherlands, to actively seek ways
to embrace the sharing economy and the start-ups driving it. In fact, the
potential for responsible sharing economy startups to contribute to more
equitable and sustainable cities led me to launch the Sharing
Accelerator Barcelona in 2016, an accelerator dedicated to fostering the
growth of responsible sharing economy startups in European cities.

Yet the collaborative economy is not just for start-ups. Multinationals
are also embracing the trend. In some cases, corporations are partnering
with successful collaborative economy start-ups. KLM Airlines partnered
with Airbnb to retrofit a plane and convert it into a luxury hotel room as
a promotional campaign. Citibank and Barclay's have sponsored the

launch and implementation of significant bikesharing programs in New York City and London, respectively.

## SUMMARY

In this chapter I sought to lay the groundwork for the emergence of urbanpreneurship in cities around the world by first contrasting innovation and entrepreneurship today with that of the past century. I introduced the Urbanpreneur Spiral for depicting the three key, overlapping trends that are most accountable for the emergence of new types of entrepreneurship occurring in urban environments. The concepts from this chapter are summarized in Figure 1.2 as well as the layout for the book.

## MOVING FORWARD

The rest of this book aims to shed light on new types of urban entrepreneurial activity. In the next chapter I will highlight the migration of tech start-ups from suburban tech parks to urban areas. Many insights for this have come from Richard Florida's recent work to track the migration of venture capital–backed technology start-ups from suburban areas into urban centers. This includes results first reported by Florida and his co-author in the *California Management Review* special issue mentioned earlier.

However, I will also be sharing insights about newer forms of urban entrepreneurship, which to date have been underreported. The first such type Pablo and I refer to as civic entrepreneurship (Chapter 3). We consider civic entrepreneurs to be a unique type of entrepreneur who has emerged in recent years focused on becoming part of the solution to local city problems utilizing the ingenuity and approach of traditional entrepreneurs. We have been tracking the emergence of civic entrepreneurs and the role cities play in fostering such innovation in their territories and I will seek to shed light on this exciting entrepreneurial form.

There is another type of urban entrepreneurship that has received the least amount of attention to date, but I believe poses the potential to be transformational in many ways. I call this group indie urbanpreneurs (Chapter 4). Indie urbanpreneurs utilize the soft and hard infrastructure in cities as a platform for creating innovations. This infrastructure can be 3D labs, co-working space, incubators, and social networks such as meetups, which are found in cities around the globe. Frequently indie urbanpreneurs do not form companies, nor do they have a start-up team

Figure 1.2  Book Layout

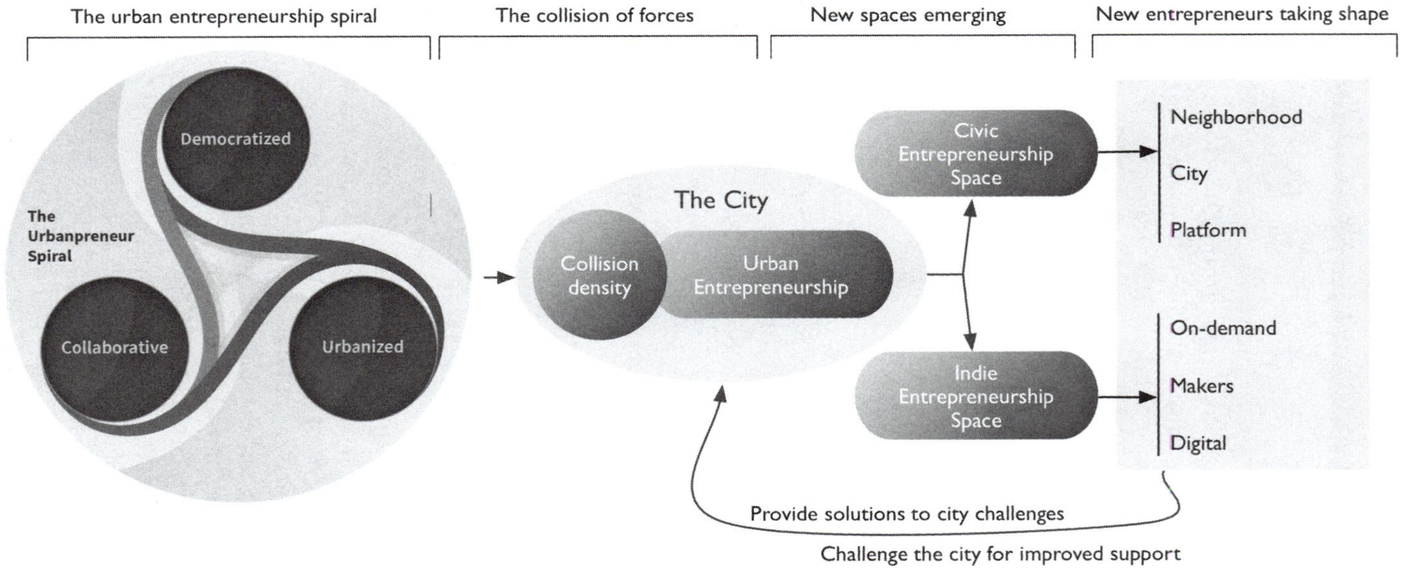

The urban entrepreneurship spiral | The collision of forces | New spaces emerging | New entrepreneurs taking shape

The Urbanpreneur Spiral

Democratized

Urbanized

Collaborative

The City

Urban Entrepreneurship

Collision density

Civic Entrepreneurship Space

Indie Entrepreneurship Space

Neighborhood

City

Platform

On-demand

Makers

Digital

Provide solutions to city challenges

Challenge the city for improved support

or employees, although they are likely to embrace collaboration. These indie urbanpreneurs are often not counted in studies of entrepreneurs because they are not producing jobs and are often not incorporated. Yet, their numbers appear to be growing.

After discussing the uniqueness and trends regarding civic entrepreneurs and indie urbanpreneurs, I will focus on the role cities, both large (Chapter 5) and small (Chapter 6), can play in fostering these forms of entrepreneurship in their territories. While urbanization has led to many efficiencies and benefits for much of the world's population, aside from the resulting strains on urban areas, the massive global migration to cities has left many small towns and smaller cities on the border of collapse. Young people are leaving in droves for the opportunities in cities. How can the lessons learned in this book help these communities stem the tide and instead attract and retain the best and brightest innovators who will guide our collaborative, democratized, and urbanized communities of the future?

I will also consider how innovation and entrepreneurship can be diffused from one city to another. My friend Jeb Brugmann published a book in 2009 entitled *Welcome to the Urban Revolution*, which articulates very well the crumbling of national boundaries and the increasing role of international cities sharing, diffusing, and competing for innovation.

Finally, Pablo and I take some liberties with the final chapter to reflect on challenges and implications for cities, innovators, entrepreneurs, and citizens of the implications of the Urbanpreneur Spiral. I personally arrive at a controversial conclusion regarding the region most likely to emerge as the strongest entrepreneurship region in the world. Hint: it is not North America.

# CHAPTER 2

## The Great Urban Migration

As has been documented by the United Nations and the media, the world is urbanizing, and fast. The implications of urbanization are vast and complex. Beyond the migration of the general population to cities, this book is dedicated to the migration of entrepreneurs and innovators to cities around the globe. While Jane Jacobs, Charles Landry, Richard Florida, and many others have long highlighted the benefits of the diversity of city life in supporting creative enterprises, many scholars, policy makers, and entrepreneurs have held the belief that high-tech entrepreneurship, and the ecosystems that commonly form to support them, must necessarily be based in suburban tech parks. Silicon Valley has served as the template and ground zero for evidence that high-tech start-ups should be located in lower-rent districts outside of urban cores. This chapter is focused on debunking this myth and demonstrating that innovation and entrepreneurship ecosystems, along with the general population, are migrating into cities.

### HOW TO BECOME THE NEXT SILICON VALLEY IS THE WRONG QUESTION!

It is no surprise why local policy makers continue to seek out ways to entice existing tech companies and new tech start-ups to their regions. The "Great Recession" the world experienced starting in 2008 with the collapse of the housing bubble drew our attention back to the reality that large banks and corporations are not reliable creators of jobs over the long term. A study by the Kauffman Foundation showed that existing large firms accounted for a net loss of 1 million jobs between 1977 and 2005.[1] Yet small companies and start-ups accounted for 8.7 million new jobs between 2011 and 2012.[2] These type of data led the Kauffman Foundation in the same 2010 report to conclude: "Startups aren't everything when it comes to job growth. They're the only thing." This is indeed a pivotal aspect of any economic cycle. Simply stated, when the economy is growing as a result of an entrepreneurial push (under the right conditions, to alleviate the concerns of institutional scholars), financiers start speculating, taking high risks that they usually can't afford and end up losing someone else's money. Managers overreact, and the economists, who could not predict this in the first place, return to market anomalies when trying to explain what happened, and then again the government calls the entrepreneurial cavalry to solve the problem and create wealth again. Economic cycles for dummies is not the main topic of this book, but rather the centrality of cities in the growth of entrepreneurship, which is relevant to anyone interested in promoting development.

In this context, I regularly find myself in discussions with local economic development agencies and city officials and mayors who seek to be the "Silicon Valley of" fill in the blank. I must admit, every time I hear this I cringe. The "build it and they will come" logic has not delivered as expected. First of all, Silicon Valley is a one-of-a-kind place that emerged through a unique combination of events and players and has developed over half a century. Silicon Valley is also home to globally leading universities like Stanford and UC Berkeley, which are virtually impossible to replicate. Someone could argue that there are indeed other Silicon Valleys, like Boston, Cambridge, or Tel Aviv, yet again they all contain impossible-to-replicate conditions, for example, Harvard, MIT, or Cambridge University, which combined produce an impressive amount of new inventions per year. Silicon Valley is also home to the highest concentration of venture capital in the world. In a tech blog musing about Berlin's ecosystem Christoph Räthke expressed his frustration about the persistent attempts by people to compare Berlin's ecosystem to that of Silicon Valley:

Silicon Valley is the result of one-of-a-kind policies, decisions and investments made over decades, some of which would be impossible or even illegal in any other country ... the state of affairs in Palo Alto, California is about as "standard" to the rest of the developed world as is the state of affairs in Pjöngjang, North Korea. Lamenting our lag behind the former is about as useful as celebrating our lead ahead of the latter.[3]

Regional policy makers continue to seek ways to become the next Silicon Valley to house these start-ups. This, I believe, is a bad idea, but not for the reasons you might have in mind. Have you actually been to Silicon Valley? Outside of a few pockets of smart urbanism, like Palo Alto, most of Silicon Valley is bland, car dependent, and lacking in any type of energy many young entrepreneurs and employees seek.

For all its power, Silicon Valley has a great weakness: the paradise Shockley found in 1956 is now one giant parking lot. San Francisco and Berkeley are great, but they're forty miles away. Silicon Valley proper is soul-crushing suburban sprawl.[4]

These words were spoken in 2006 by famed start-up investor, Paul Graham, best known for cofounding the Y-Combinator, one of North America's first tech accelerator programs.

Silicon Valley is not all it is cracked up to be and, in my opinion, is no longer the desired future for innovators and entrepreneurs. As an entre-preneur leading 3rdWhale, a mobile company dedicated to the green con-sumer, I was invited to participate in a pitch competition along with 45 other entrepreneurs at Plug and Play in Sunnyvale. Despite having a PhD in entrepreneurship and having taught dozens of entrepreneurship courses and advised hundreds of start-ups, I found myself quite nervous as I was randomly picked to be the first entrepreneur to give a 2-minute pitch in front of dozens of a half-dozen leading Silicon Valley venture capitalists. The top five pitches were to be selected to also give a 10-minute pitch at the end of the day. Although 3rdWhale was a very early-stage company with a niche green focus, we were lucky enough to be selected for the next pitch. I was so inspired by that experience that I decided to pay for regular access to Plug and Play and return from Vancouver on a monthly basis in hopes of raising venture capital funding.

I probably returned to Silicon Valley 10 times between 2007 and 2008. With all apologies to the impressive innovators, entrepreneurs, and investors who call the Valley home, and notwithstanding some nice examples of smarter urbanism like much of Palo Alto, most of the Valley is really quite dreary. Some monolithic single- or two-story office buildings go on forever. Good luck getting around without a car. Walkability, forget about it. Silicon Valley is as far away as possible from the utopian creative class city Richard Florida identified more than a dozen years ago. Thus, it comes as no surprise that Florida's recent research has found that the tech start-up community, just like the popula-tion at large, is urbanizing in big numbers.

There are clear signs, however, that entrepreneurs, including those in the tech sectors, will increasingly migrate to urban locations. Just recently, for example, the new giant and still entrepreneurial Uber, instead of building a trendy "campus" in the middle of Silicon Valley, closed a deal to buy the historic Sears building in the heart of downtown Oakland. In research Florida and his team at the Martin Prosperity Institute revealed recently, two urban districts of San Francisco, Portero Hill and Rincon Hill, have experienced more venture capital infusion than Mountain View, one of the classic suburban tech park communities of Silicon Valley. The Boston Consulting Group confirmed this in their study that demonstrated that more venture capital money is being invested in San Francisco and Oakland area tech companies ($7 billion in 2012) than in Silicon Valley ($4 billion in 2012).[5] Not only are more start-ups being founded, and funded, in San Francisco every year, but former Silicon Valley–based heavyweights like Twitter and Yelp have relocated to San Francisco to attract and retain younger employees seeking more pedestrian friendly, culturally dynamic environs. Jack Dorsey, Twitter's co-founder, tweeted, of course, his pleasure with being located in the heart of San Francisco: "I love the idea of an urban corporate campus with all the energy and variety that provides." Dorsey went on to found a new tech company, Square, and also chose San Francisco over the Valley to locate his growing start-up with 400 employees. The co-founder and CEO of Zendesk, Mikkel Svane, chose to locate the company in Tenderloin, a struggling neighborhood in San Francisco offering tax incentives for companies to locate and support the regeneration process because:

After co-founding the company in Copenhagen in 2007, Silicon Valley was never an option when he decided to take the firm stateside. He cites the urban buzz of San Francisco, but also says it had the kinds of communities and services better suited to his wife, who is deaf. He didn't want to "isolate her in the boonies. We're city people."[6]

Based on research from Colliers International reported in CNN, 60 percent of all commercial leases in San Francisco in 2015 were to tech companies.[7] This trend of tech entrepreneurs moving to or starting up in urban environments is not unique to San Francisco. This trend appears to be global. New York City, London, Berlin, Barcelona, Buenos Aires, Seattle, Seoul, and many other cities around the globe have witnessed an influx of tech-based entrepreneurs. Of course, there is a lot a city can do to encourage this activity, which is why Chapters 5 and 6 are dedicated exclusively to exploring what cities are doing or could do to accelerate this process.

This urban migration is not all good, since the infusion of higher paying jobs into the city is pricing out lower-income people from the urban core. The goal for cities should be to strive for some aspect of "gentrification without displacement" discussed toward the end of the book. Indeed, the immediate reaction after Uber's announcement wasn't all excitement. According to *Wired* magazine:

The fear, it seemed, was that a company of Uber's caliber moving into Oakland might mean the same gentrification that San Francisco has faced—the displacement of bodegas and rent-controlled apartments in favor of luxury condos and artisanal toast shops.[8]

## EVEN SUBURBAN TECH PARKS ARE URBANIZING

Interestingly, even suburban tech parks are trying to embrace urbanism as a way to retain their current base while also attracting new tenants. In September 2015 I was invited to join other urban innovation experts in helping Berlin launch the Creating Urban Tech Event. I took the opportunity to visit with various stakeholders in the thriving innovation ecosystem Berlin offers. I visited Aldershof, a tech park about 30 minutes from the city center. I was meeting with Ramin Mokhtari, cofounder and CEO of a venture-backed smart cities company in the afternoon. Having had bad experiences showing up at other such tech parks around the globe, I had no idea if I would find any place to eat within walking distance of the train station. To my surprise, I noticed some play areas, a grocery store, residences, a park, bike paths, and yes, a handful of restaurants. During a later conversation with Cornelia Yzer, Berlin's Senator tasked with leading the Department for Economics, Technology and Research, informed me that the Aldershof had gone through an urbanization transformation due to demand from, guess who, the younger generation of entrepreneurs and staff with offices located in the park. Consistent with the broader trends of urban migration, as the tech park filled with startups, demand for parks, schools, commercial areas, and other aspects of urban life emerged.

Perhaps the most important example of this transformation is the one under way with the Research Triangle Park (RTP) in North Carolina. This part of North Carolina is home to several world-class research universities such as the University of North Carolina (Chapel Hill), Duke University, and North Carolina State. University and government visionaries imagined a high-tech suburban research park in the early 1950s that would attract tech companies from around North America and of course house spinoffs from the local universities. By the end of the 1950s RTP succeeded in attracting its first five companies. Over the decades RTP grew continuously and today it houses approximately 200 companies and 50,000 tech workers.

Yet in recent years, RTP has begun to reflect the broader trends of citizens and entrepreneurs seeking more urban environments. As such, RTP leaders have embarked on an urban transformation project, towards something the Brookings Institution refers to as an "urbanized science park." The Research Triangle Foundation recently unveiled a 50-year transformation plan complete with significant retail and residential areas. In hopes of stemming recent tenant losses to more urban environments, in 2014, the foundation announced plans for a 100-acre expansion that could generate up to 100,000 new jobs and convert the suburban park into a more vibrant live-work tech cluster capable of attracting and retaining the graduates of the nearby research universities as well as tech founders and workers from around the country and the world. "North Carolina's Research Triangle Park, perhaps the 20th century's most iconic research and development campus, is the strongest validation of this (urbanized science park) model."[9]

While suburban tech parks are urbanizing, the bigger trend remains the migration of entrepreneurs from suburban areas to more urban environments filled with not only a high concentration of start-ups but also coffee shops, restaurants, cultural activities, denser housing, good transit, and walkability.

## FROM "SOUL-CRUSHING" SUBURBAN TECH PARKS TO URBAN INNOVATION DISTRICTS

The idea of replicating Silicon Valley is slowly giving way to a smarter form of housing and growing a local start-up community: the innovation district. The idea behind innovation districts is for cities to create a set of incentives for start-ups and established companies to set up shop in dense urban environments. More often than not, these innovation districts are targeted as part of an urban regeneration project. Views over results are still conflicting. Some argue that it is part of the natural evolution of cities, and the newcomers and entrepreneurs will settle in replacing eventually the current floating population full of contractors whose actual home is over 100 miles away. Others, however, have used recent (yet not necessarily compelling) evidence to argue that these new developments are completely disconnected from the actual fiber of transit, poor infrastructure, and an overall lack of amenities. ⸱s Aires city planners, led by visionaries such as senior architect l Chain, envisioned a transformation of this neighborhood by ⸱ving the local infrastructure while offering incentives such as a ⸱e zone (city taxes only). The city expanded a metro line to reach ⸱re of the Distrito and began redevelopment of some key physical ⸱ructure. Buenos Aires also implemented a cool iconic building to innovative events related to the information and communication ⸱logy (ICT) sector such as hackathons and pitch events, an expan- ⸱f the top local engineering university and ICT incubators. At the ⸱f this writing the Distrito Tecnologico, modeled after Barcelona's ⸱oused 194 ICT companies employing 11,000 workers.

⸱lellín has also embraced the innovation district approach. This is ⸱ surprising given the city's reputation for embracing innovation in ⸱as become one of the most impressive city transformations in the past ⸱y. The city has been working with several international consultancies ⸱ing Carlo Ratti and his peers at MIT in Boston, to develop and imple- ⸱Medellínnovation District to support the growth of tech companies in ⸱y while also helping to regenerate the northern part of the city. In the ⸱of Carlo Ratti's team: "Underlying the plan is a network of parks, pub- ⸱ces, and pedestrian oriented streets that will create an open, healthy ⸱oductive environment. Carabobo becomes the 'main street' for major ⸱nies as well as the shopping and social life of the District. Research ⸱ducational facilities are clustered along a spine connecting ⸱rsity of Antioquia to the river. Finally, places to live and work—in ⸱nterprises—are woven into the neighborhoods, with new facilities ⸱rting public education, training, and engagement anchoring the ⸱t."[11]

⸱re are other similar movements afoot to embrace the role of cities in ⸱novation and entrepreneurship agenda. In 2005, the UK government ⸱ned a program called Science Cities whereby the goal is to facilitate ⸱tion and entrepreneurship in Birmingham, Bristol, Manchester, ⸱astle, Nottingham, and York through collaborations with universities, ⸱governments, and the private sector. I have heard rumors that the sci- ⸱cities initiative emerged as a response to the already crowded ⸱ridge (suburban) Science Parks. Evidence is stacking up. While the ⸱pproach focused on city-wide innovation ecosystems, and innovation ⸱ts encourage clustering of innovation activity in one area in the hopes ⸱ieving local regeneration and network effects, Boston is now experi- ⸱ng with Neighborhood Innovation Districts with the idea of distribut- ⸱novation across the whole city.

the city. They are likely to follow the prevailing aı
but have been unable to get intertwined with (o
historically rooted social-cultural dynamics of a
embedded innovation districts are here to stay a
the other, have gained traction and most import
policy-making arena.

Barcelona was one of the first cities in the wor
cept of an innovation district. Known as 22@, this
trict had fallen into disrepair as industrial operati
out of the city toward the middle and end of tl
Seeking an infusion of private investment and
start-up community in the city, Barcelona's City
idea of turning this derelict district into a high-ı
and education. They started by investing heav
throughout the district and constructing a few ic
to house city innovation hubs, incubators, and sc
bet the farm, investing over 180 million euros sii
in 2000. Barcelona also committed to building aı
able and social housing in the district. In a study cᴄ
its founding, the city reports that 22@ now hosts m
nies and 56,000 employees.[10]

While some companies previously existed in Bar
Europe, and have been enticed to move to the dist
access to the digital infrastructure, or collaborati
other like-minded companies, the city reports that
nies are founded in 22@. One of the beauties of
that they frequently seek to support urban regenera
borhoods as opposed to locate them in high-rent
suburban tech parks. Because land values are usual
in urban areas, cities are often able to support the ᴄ
able housing. Barcelona's success inspired similar
cities such as Buenos Aires, Medellín, and Bostᴄ
cussed further in the final chapters regarding what
more entrepreneurs to their locales.

While each has its own spin, most innovation
items in common. They are regularly built in abaı
downtown core. They are also generally co-located
sities or are used to attract branches of existing univ
urban areas. The Distrito Tecnologico ("Technoloɡ
Aires provides such an example. The neighborhoo
los Patricios, was a historically poor part of the city,

publi
Buen
Dani
impr
tax-f
the ᴄ
infra
hous
tech
sion
time
22@,

Mᴇ
hard
what
centᴜ
inclᴜ
ment
the ᴄ
word
lic sp
and ı
comฺ
and
Univ
new
suppᴇ
Distrʲ

Th
the iı
launᴄ
inve
New
local
ence
Cam
UK a
distrʲ
of ac
menᴋ
ing iı

Speaking of Boston, the city's innovation hub was once Route 128, another suburban tech park, similar to RTP. Route 128 is a beltway circling the city of Boston and providing an unnatural barrier between the city and the suburbs. Like RTP, Route 128 also benefitted from university spin-offs, in this case primarily from Harvard and Boston, although Greater Boston is home to some 74 colleges and universities. In the late 1950s Route 128 housed about 100 companies and 17,000 employees. The region continued to grow through the 1990s. However, in what now probably reads like a broken record, the trends in urbanization of the tech sector placed strains on Route 128 as an innovation hub. Key players in Route 128 have also actively pursued the urbanized science park concept. But Boston's innovation and tech sector could not be confined to a highway corridor. In 2010, Boston's then mayor, Thomas Menino, was also inspired by the success of Barcelona's 22@ district. He developed a vision for a new Innovation District as part of an urban regeneration project in Boston's South Waterfront. Boston's Innovation District, and its latest initiatives to create neighborhood innovation districts, will be discussed in Chapter 5.

In 2014, the Brookings Institution released a report entitled "The Rise of Innovation Districts: A New Geography of Innovation in America." In this report, the Brookings Institution documented the rising trends of innovation districts around the globe, and particularly in the United States in cities such as Atlanta, Baltimore, Buffalo, Cambridge, Cleveland, Detroit, Houston, Philadelphia, Pittsburgh, St. Louis, and San Diego. On page 1 of their report, they highlight the uniqueness of innovation districts as an economic development tool for cities:

Innovation districts represent a radical departure from traditional economic development. Unlike customary urban revitalization efforts that have emphasized the commercial aspects of development (e.g., housing, retail, sports stadiums), innovation districts help their city and metropolis move up the value chain of global competitiveness by growing the firms, networks, and traded sectors that drive broad-based prosperity. Instead of building isolated science parks, innovation districts focus extensively on creating a dynamic physical realm that strengthens proximity and knowledge spillovers. Rather than focus on discrete industries, innovation districts represent an intentional effort to create new products, technologies and market solutions through the convergence of disparate sectors and specializations (e.g., information technology and bioscience, energy, or education).[12]

In short, the Brookings Institution's report on innovation districts stated, "the trend is to nurture living, breathing communities rather than sterile compounds of research silos."

Growing technology firms once required massive amounts of physical space to store their hardware, servers, and lab space. Because technology has gotten cheaper (sometimes "free" in the case of open source software, for example) and start-ups can increasingly use the cloud to store data instead of in-house servers, the need for tech companies to be in suburban areas has been reduced. The rapidly declining costs of technology also results in increased access to larger pools of entrepreneurs than before and minimizes the need for venture capital, at least in some cases. Pools of entrepreneurs are not only larger but more diverse and spreading throughout Chris Anderson's "Long Tail," where instead of insular big hits, such as the iPod, there are a huge number of niches reaching customers unhappy with the one-size-fits-all idea. All of these trends reinforce one of the components of the Urbanpreneur Spiral, that is, the democratization of innovation and technology. As inputs into start-ups move toward free, distributed, and virtual, the need to find large spaces outside of cities to locate growing start-ups is diminishing. And so is the need to have massive amounts of venture capital for the early-stage start-up scene.

## FROM BUREAUCRATIC CITIES TO SMART CITIES

With 1.3 million newbies each week, many global cities are straining to meet the demands on infrastructure, education, energy, and food systems caused by the steady in-migration. Imagine how much food, water, energy, education, and housing cities will need to satisfy the needs of 500+ million more people, who demand Western standards just because they moved to the city. Economic fluctuations in recent years have only exacerbated the problem as cities struggle to maintain their tax base. As a result, cities are increasingly turning to the private sector, and to citizens directly, to help reinvent the cities of the future. While there are numerous terms for this evolution, many experts in the field of urban planning and innovation have referred to this movement as smart cities. I have been studying the smart cities revolution for several years and in fact started benchmarking global and regional smart cities in Fast Company starting in 2011.

As part of this work, I began reviewing best practices in smart cities and eventually developed a tool I refer to as the Smart Cities Wheel. It contains six key components: Smart Economy, Smart Government, Smart People, Smart Living, Smart Mobility, and Smart Environment. Each component of the wheel (included in the Preface to this book) contains three subcomponents from which I subsequently developed a set of indicators. In 2013, I used 28 indicators as proxies for measuring the 6 components and 18 subcomponents of the wheel. In 2014, I worked with a small group of global smart cities experts to expand the indicator set to 62. I was able to obtain complete data for only 11 global cities, so I placed the cities in three categories: Pioneering (Barcelona, Copenhagen, Helsinki, Singapore, Vancouver, Vienna); Emerging (Brisbane, Los Angeles, Montreal), and Next Stage (Bogotá, Lima).[13]

Smart cities are a complicated phenomenon because cities are systems of systems, which result in layers of complexity that need to work with each other continuously to avoid collapse. In fact, there has been a lot of research from academics in the past few decades using complexity theories in an effort to understand cities as complex systems. That is to say that there are several overlapping systems operating in cities simultaneously, such as transport systems, food systems, social systems, ecological systems, and of course innovation and entrepreneurial ecosystems. It is a never-ending story where everything is connected to everything, and the performance of a system relies on the performance of the other. This is something that is difficult to admit, but my admiration for mayors (or pity for that matter) has grown in recent years. I was surprised when I saw the book from Benjamin Barber came out a few years ago, *If Mayors Ruled the World*. Like my friend Jeb Brugmann, in *Welcome to the Urban Revolution*, Barber recognizes that the world is increasingly made up of interconnected cities more so than nation-states. And that cities, and the mayors who lead them, are increasingly driving the global innovation and sustainability agenda.

The smart cities movement, at its core, is about how cities can embrace innovation in everything they do. More innovative and efficient in the use of public funds, more innovative in their willingness to experiment, more innovative in supporting citizen cocreation, more innovative in embracing the power of ICTs, and more innovative in their support for urban entrepreneurial ecosystems.

Alongside my colleagues Esteve Almirall and Henry Chesbrough, the "Father of Open Innovation" based at UC Berkeley, I was the lead guest editor for a special issue of the *California Management Review* dedicated to the role of cities as a platform for innovation. In our call for papers, we summarized the challenges and opportunities for smarter cities this way:

In short, the majority of the world's population is living in cities, putting pressure on cities to be smarter in the provision of basic needs while trying to stimulate the local economy. Emerging collaborative economy concepts such as carsharing, crowdfunding, crowdsourcing, big data and open data are merging with the smart cities movement to create an interesting mashup and leading to new forms of innovation ecosystems in urban environments.

It is clear that tech entrepreneurs are increasingly turning to cities, to be part of innovation districts or to just plug into the overall entrepreneurial ecosystem found in cities around the globe. Yet there is still a lot to be learned about the emerging urban tech ecosystems. Entrepreneurship scholars have spent decades exploring public policy tools, economic outcomes, and entrepreneurial behavior associated with suburban tech parks. In fact, the very first academic study I was part of during my PhD program at the University of Colorado was focused on studying the factors that were driving the growth of the tech-based entrepreneurial ecosystem in the Boulder area. We were not focused on the urban space, but rather the greater Boulder arena primarily in the corridor between Denver and Boulder, Colorado. In that study, published in 2004, after surveying more than 100 tech entrepreneurs and interviewing 15 more, we found that social networks, the University of Colorado, governmental regulations and support, professional services, capital sources, access to talent, the presence of large technology firms, the physical infrastructure of the region, and the culture toward entrepreneurship were all critical factors in the success of the region's tech-based entrepreneurial ecosystem.

However, we were studying closed innovation and entrepreneurial ecosystems, which made a lot of sense more than a decade ago. Many other scholars have conducted similar studies in other regions of the world and also found similar results. The question now, however, is what factors contribute to vibrant urban tech-based entrepreneurial ecosystems? Surely some factors carry over, but others may not, or at least would be weighted differently in modern urban ecosystems. For example, I have already documented what I believe to be a decreased importance for the presence of traditional venture capital in facilitating urban technology entrepreneurship due to the democratization of innovation and the increased use of crowdfunding. Also, in our Boulder study, physical infrastructure was identified by only 20 percent of the founders as an important reason for locating in the region. Urban tech entrepreneurs in modern cities are surely looking at physical infrastructure like public transit, cycling infrastructure, and digital infrastructure like high-speed bandwidth as factors in deciding where to move. Having recently delivered a keynote speech at Kansas City's Gigabit Summit, I can state with certainty that Kansas City is banking on the fact that by being the first city in the United States to partner with Google to install Google Fiber throughout the city, Kansas City will gain major benefits in growing the local and immigrant tech entrepreneurial community.

Luckily, early research is being conducted on urban tech ecosystems so some results are starting to emerge regarding features that are key to successful urban technology ecosystems. In 2015, the Global Startup Ecosystem Index was released by the Startup Genome initiative as a follow-up to their first ranking in 2012. Their research uncovered five key factors influencing regional and urban entrepreneurial ecosystem performance. They included performance, funding market reach, talent, and start-up experience.

After crunching the numbers from 50,000 global start-ups, the Genome team identified the top 20 performing entrepreneurial ecosystems (numbers in parentheses indicate the 2012 ranking). These included, in order: 1. Silicon Valley (1), 2. New York City (5), 3. Los Angeles (3), 4. Boston (6), 5. Tel Aviv (2), 6. London (7), 7. Chicago (10), 8. Seattle (4), 9. Berlin (15), 10. Singapore (17), 11. Paris (11), 12. São Paulo (13), 13. Moscow (14), 14. Austin (New), 15. Bangalore (19), 16. Sydney (12), 17. Toronto (8), 18. Vancouver (9), 19. Amsterdam (New), 20. Montreal (New).

While the Genome research was quite useful and certainly generated plenty of media attention, it was not exclusively focused on urban tech entrepreneurial ecosystems as they often incorporate a more regional approach to evaluating entrepreneurial ecosystems. Fortunately, more recently, the World Bank has been doing a deep dive into urban tech innovation ecosystems. After conducting a review of the current literature and completing a pilot study of New York City's tech ecosystem, the World Bank started to publish some of their results.[14] I was also fortunate to receive a draft copy of their first report for which some of the following information is drawn.

The World Bank's researchers, led by Victor Mulas, developed a framework consisting of five elements they deem to be critical to the success of urban tech ecosystems. These include people, infrastructure, enabling environment, economic assets, and networking assets. Since I have discussed people and infrastructure in detail above, I will focus on the new items. *Economic assets* include aspects such as diversity of industries, businesses and sectors, universities and R&D facilities, and early-stage investment accessibility. *Enabling environment* refers to the role of local government in supporting the tech sector. *Networking assets* refers to the overlapping sets of social networks and activities that combine to facilitate interdisciplinary and often random interactions among techies, investors, artists, inventors, and others in the ecosystem.

What the World Bank's early research is finding is that networking assets provide the glue to the other components of the ecosystem and may be the single-most important part of a vibrant urban tech ecosystem. I believe this particular topic, which I like to refer to as collision density, is particularly interesting as it has been emerging as a possible clue to what differentiates successful urban ecosystems from undeveloped ones.

## COLLISION DENSITY

The World Bank report breaks down networking assets into five categories: community-building events, skills training events, collaboration spaces, and mentor networks. The idea behind collision density is that the more opportunities for cross-disciplinary interaction, the more potential for breakthrough innovations. Corporations have long understood this and of course seek to find ways to avoid silo-based innovation projects. Even going back to Schumpeter, one of the world's most recognized early economics scholars to recognize the potential of entrepreneurs to transform economies, clearly articulated the role of entrepreneurs in making previously unrecognized connections between disparate fields. Despite the inherent logic that cities where more opportunities for interaction among experts from diverse fields will have more vibrant tech-based entrepreneurial ecosystems, this concept has barely been studied by entrepreneurship scholars or discussed in urban innovation circles.

The first time I ever heard the term *collision density* in reference to entrepreneurship was in 2013 in reference to Kansas City's aspirations to turn their Google Fiber infrastructure into a driving force for fostering a world-class urban tech ecosystem.[15] So I was pleasantly surprised to see that the World Bank is already working on how to measure collision density. I believe it is important to note that many pundits predicted that the ICT revolution would actually reduce the dependence on physical interactions with a local entrepreneurial ecosystem. After all, if you can have a great idea in your home or office in London, sketch something out, and outsource the development of a prototype to India and launch the beta in New York, without ever leaving your office, then why do you need physical interactions with artists, inventors, programmers, and so on, which are more likely to occur in cities? The answer is that most radical, or disruptive, innovations do not develop this way. They require random and planned physical interactions with diverse individuals on a regular basis.

Dennis Crowley co-founded and grew a social Web-based app called Dodgeball with Alex Rainert out of NYU, which they sold to Google.

Crowley and Rainert were brought into Google with the acquisition. However, in 2009, Dodgeball was "turned off" by Google. Crowley mostly used Dodgeball to coordinate his own social life so he was keen to find a way to recreate something similar so that he and his friends could still coordinate their social lives using technology. Crowley's next venture, Foursquare, sought to recreate the social networking ability of Dodgeball but with mobile technology at its core. The story of how Foursquare came together is a prime example of collision density at work.

Crowley was living in New York, working at another tech start-up called Area/Code. Area/Code was an early-stage start-up based in a co-work facility. Naveen Salvadurai happened to be working in the same co-work facility but with a different start-up. They soon realized that together they could bring concepts from Dodgeball back to life, but make it better with the growing power of smartphones and the ability to develop apps for the iPhone, Android phones, and other platforms. Thus, the pair who had collided in the tech scene within a co-work facility in New York City, coincidentally the focus of the World Bank's pilot study, joined forces to create Foursquare and agreed to introduce an early version at the annual South by Southwest (SXSW) tech event in Austin in 2009. While the original goal of Foursquare was to keep the essence of Dodgeball alive while enabling Crowley and others to continue to engage with the locations where they were living or visiting, Foursquare had 10 million users and raised $50 million in venture capital in 2011 at a valuation of $600 million.

This chapter was dedicated to exploring the continued urbanization of the planet and the migration not just of citizens but of high- and low-tech start-ups in urban centers. Given the strong connection between high-growth, high-tech start-ups and economic development and job growth, it is no surprise that this particular shift from suburban to urban tech ecosystems has started to attract significant interest. This is an important development in the global tech entrepreneurship community and of course has significant implications for local and regional governments. However, having worked in smart cities and urban innovation the past several years, I have come to realize there are other emerging trends shaping entrepreneurship in urban settings that deserve attention from entrepreneurship scholars, local governments, entrepreneurs, and other participants of urban entrepreneurial ecosystems. Specifically the two "new" forms of urban entrepreneurship arenas addressed in the following two chapters are civic entrepreneurship and a new type of independent entrepreneurship leveraging collision density and other aspects of the "invisible infrastructure" of cities, which I refer to as indie urbanpreneurship arena. In both of them, I have identified a number of types, each of which represents distinct forms of entrepreneurial behavior, arguably shaped by their emergent inter-actions with cities. While current data lead us only to preliminary conclu-sions, I believe that the migration of the tech scene into urban areas is having positive spillover effects (i.e., positive externalities) with the growth of these newer forms of urbanpreneurship. Time—and further research I am conducting with Pablo and other colleagues—will tell.

# CHAPTER 3

## Emergence of the Civic Entrepreneurship Space

On October 18, 2009, Martine Postma launched the world's first Repair Café in Amsterdam. Her idea was to support local sustainability and community building by bringing people together to fix things that were laying around people's homes and likely headed for a landfill. Recognizing the decline in repair shops for things like broken toasters and torn couches, Martine believed community members with the capability to fix things would be willing to donate their time to help out other local residents recover their nearly discarded items. The Repair Café was not conceived of as a permanent physical location, but instead as a rotating monthly event hosted by different cafes, commercial enterprise, or other supporters. The idea took off. As of June 2015, there were more than 700 official Repair Cafés in cities around the globe, including one founded by Pablo and his wife in Santiago in early 2015. I consider this a classic example of civic entrepreneurship, leveraging sharing economy approaches, albeit with no money exchanging hands. This chapter is dedicated to exploring the evolution of cities, the economics of cities, and placemaking, which have combined to support the growth of the civic entrepreneurship space and of several types of entrepreneurs within it.

Entrepreneurs working in the civic space seek to improve the quality of life where they live through entrepreneurial behavior. Thus, instead of having a primarily outward, export-focused business model, civic entrepreneurs prefer to look for problems in their neighborhoods and cities and to find entrepreneurial solutions for improving local quality of life. Points of Light, out of Atlanta, launched an accelerator for civic ventures in 2011. Code for America launched a civic venture accelerator out of San Francisco in 2012. Another civic accelerator, Tuml, was also founded in San Francisco by graduates from MIT's Sloan Management School. Also in 2012, Avina Americas, Fundacion Avina, and Omidyar Network collaborated to create a Civic Innovation Accelerator Fund of 1.6 million (USD) to "bridge the gap between civic movements and technology, identifying and supporting the implementation of technological innovations that accelerate collective strategies for social change, accountability, and transparency, particularly in urban areas of Latin America" (Appcivico.net).

A local entrepreneur and the city of Jackson Hole created a sustainable agri-business to increase community participation. A group of entrepreneurial moms and the city of Bristol (UK) are reopening public spaces for children to play on the street. The city of San Francisco has an Office of Civic Innovation while the city of Boston has the office of New Urban Mechanics. Civic crowdfunding platforms such as Neighbor.ly, Spacehive, and Citizinvestor have emerged to support neighborhood projects and civic ventures around the globe. In order to understand the emergence of civic entrepreneurship, it is important to explore the evolutionary nature of cities, the economics of cities, and placemaking.

## EVOLUTIONARY NATURE OF CITIES

In the past decade, urban scholars have increasingly looked to the physical sciences to understand the nature and evolution of cities. In his 2009 book *City Planning, Design and Evolution*, Stephen Marshall, professor in the Bartlett School of Planning at University College London, suggests that we need to reframe our thinking around cities. Rather than viewing cities as a single unified (corporate) object, Marshall implores us to view them as collective entities comprised of many individual but overlapping components of ecosystems that are not as much intentionally developed but evolve over time. This evolutionary view of cities, grounded in biology, has also been expanded by others to embrace the idea that cities are really complex systems of systems similar to other evolving biological systems in the natural world.

Michael Batty, another professor of Planning at University College London, has been spearheading efforts to introduce the "new science of cities" leveraging complexity science, which originated from the biological sciences. In his 2013 book *The New Science of Cities*, Batty encourages urbanists to view cities as complex evolutionary systems of systems including transportation, urban food distribution systems, retail and commerce systems, information and communication systems, housing systems, and ecological systems, which are not static but rather evolve through intended and unintended action by government, residents, organizations, and tourists.

We can think of cities as made up of both soft and hard infrastructure, which evolve over time. Hard infrastructure are things like roads, transit systems, buildings, high-speed Internet networks, and energy distribution systems. Soft infrastructure are things like culture, health care, education, and accessibility of experts and investors in a city. Both hard and soft infrastructure evolve in cities over time, not necessarily at the same rate, and often in overlapping ways. As a city's hard infrastructure expands, more residents and companies become part of the city's fabric, attracting more soft infrastructure as well. Yet, the rapid urbanization of cities around the globe is often occurring at a pace too fast for the hard and soft infrastructure to keep up with the demands placed on them. This leads to problems with access to energy, clean drinking water, housing, public transit, food, jobs, and basic services such as quality education and health care. Local governments have been trying to introduce new policies, such as rezoning low-density neighborhoods and increasing public transit infrastructure to relieve the stress on soft and hard infrastructure. Yet there are numerous barriers, including sizeable economic barriers, for local governments to go it alone in ensuring stable and ideally improved quality of life for citizens in the face of increased population.

## ECONOMICS OF MODERN CITIES

As has been discussed throughout this book, the world is urbanizing, placing significant pressure on urban infrastructure and support systems. The dynamics of urban economics are complex given the relationship of cities to their federal government, the jurisdictional borders created, the varying roles of regional governments, metropolitan governments, and the differential powers and expectations of city governments in the provision of energy, public transit and transportation, building codes, ability to tax property and consumption, and much more. In short, there is no easy way to generalize the dynamics of how cities are financed.

Many cities around the globe rely heavily on property taxes to finance local government operation and the provision of services to citizens. In 2012, 47.6 percent of New York City's tax revenue came from property tax, while local income tax represented 31.6 percent and 17.2 percent from consumption and use taxes (sales tax, utility tax, cigarette taxes, and hotel) (the remaining 3.6 percent came from other tax sources).[1] However, the heavy reliance on property tax to serve the needs of growing urban populations is fraught with problems. One problem is that as cities have sprawled, particularly in North and South America, but around the globe as well, municipal governments need to offer significant infrastructure to people who do not even pay property taxes to the city (often referred to as free riders) because they live in other municipalities but commute regularly to the larger city for work and leisure.

Another related problem is that cities are struggling to keep the cost of housing low enough to attract and retain the entire creative class such as artists, teachers, and many others critical to the success of their economies and culture. Increasing property tax only serves to exacerbate displacement from gentrification. A recent report from Calgary's Chamber of Commerce articulates some of these critical problems with the overreliance on property tax to fund city operations:

Property taxes, however, tend to be unresponsive to economic changes. Given Calgary's relatively high population growth, the high reliance on property tax does a poor job of accommodating the demands a rapidly increasing population puts on existing infrastructure and public services. Property taxes are also troublesome because they do not necessarily reflect an individual's ability to pay, how much services are consumed, and does not account for free riders. In turn, the property tax is an inefficient way to pay for services.[2]

Another important source of income for cities comes in the form of income tax on local businesses. As cities increasingly become attractive locations for large and small firms, revenue streams from income tax on these businesses can also become an important contributor to a local government's capability to finance hard and soft infrastructure. Yet, this too has the potential to be unproductive as high rates of sales tax can dissuade companies from moving into cities. Just as state and regional governments have been offering tax incentives to attract manufacturing firms such as automobile production, cities too are reducing, or waiving, local income tax altogether, in the hopes of attracting job-creating enterprises in their jurisdictions. Thus, local income tax on businesses may not yield sufficient income for cities to meet the needs of their growing populations.

Back in 2004, the city of Salford in the UK teamed up with the Peel Group, the Central Salford Urban Regeneration Company and the Northwest Regional Development Agency to develop MediaCityUK. The original idea was to relocate 1,800 BBC employees from the London offices to Manchester. This made sense to the BBC since London was already crowded and spending per head was low in northern England, and to the cities of Manchester and Salford because it meant more opportunities for locals. By 2012, over 1,100 BBC staff relocated to Salford Quays. The project gained traction and 10 years later the 200-acre site is home to a wide range of businesses from major corporations to start-ups, including the BBC, ITV, and the University of Salford, and nearly 40 service companies. The migration to Salford would require housing and leisure solutions, so the site also offers apartments to buy or rent, serviced apartments and hotels, and conference space capable of holding events for up to 6,500 people.

Although impressive for just 10 years of history, this project brought to light one of the major issues with cities becoming attractive magnets for companies. In 2012, a report showed that MediaCityUK did create over 700 new jobs, but only 24 went to people from Salford, despite a total of 3,172 applications. Of course, I am not considering here the ones that worked in the construction of MediaCityUK. A total of 250 out of the 700 new jobs were given to people living in Greater Manchester and the majority were given to people from outside the region.[3] I think it is fascinating how projects like MediaCityUK have the potential to revitalize cities, but there are several issues cities need to be aware of, because these emergent concerns can detract from their achievements.

As articulated in Calgary's report, one big concern about property taxes (as well as income and consumption taxes) is their lack of responsiveness to economic fluctuations. Many cities have struggled mightily since the Great Recession in large part because of their overreliance of taxes on local residents to fund operations. When property values plummet, homeowners struggle to pay their mortgages and their property taxes go unpaid. Residents lose their jobs, meaning lower income and sales tax revenues too. This vicious cycle led to the bankruptcy of Detroit, Michigan; San Bernardino, California; Mammoth Lakes, California; and Boise County, Idaho, among other North American cities between 2010 and 2014.

One area of hope in new city revenue comes in the form of increasing fees and taxes for undesirable behaviors, which can serve as an incentive to encourage cultural change. Singapore provides a great example in their impressive use of dynamic electronic road pricing (ERP). In hopes of dissuading residents and visitors from regularly using single-occupancy vehicles, Singapore implemented ERP to manage congestion and average travel speeds throughout the city. The ERP system is dynamic in that the tariff evolves in real time based on actual congestion levels. Singapore generates about 150 million (Singapore dollars) per year in revenue from the ERP system, which is directly reinvested in public transit infrastructure. Singapore also has a very sizable deterrent to car ownership in the first place, via very high vehicle permit fees. By 2012, the fees for obtaining a vehicle permit for purchasing a new vehicle rose to nearly 70,000 (USD).

While some may argue the fees associated with vehicle ownership and operation in Singapore are draconian, these programs not only provide an important source of income for the local government but also serve as a significant deterrent to vehicle ownership, reducing congestion and contamination in the city-state.

## PLACEMAKING

The previous sections discussed the evolutionary nature, and the economics, of cities. This section is focused on the concept of placemaking and its growing importance for citizens and citizens in modern cities. Perhaps no single author, or book, has had more impact on urbanist thinking than that of Jane Jacobs's 1961 masterpiece entitled *The Death and Life of Great American Cities*.[4] In this seminal book, Jacobs bemoans the car-centric top-down planning regime that existed at the time, and unfortunately still permeates throughout many cities, particularly in North America. Jacobs suggested that the voice of the individual citizen was lost in the top-down planning approaches. Moreover, Jacobs argued that local knowledge about place was missing in the grand visions for cities, often built around the car, not the person. More recently, Richard Sennett, the famed sociologist currently based at Cambridge University in the UK, has reinforced the failure of modern planning practices to embrace the individual. Just like modern labor seem to corrode character, as Richard Sennett argues, the way cities have been thought and built seems to erode tradition, identity, and the human side of humans.

The art of designing cities declined drastically in the middle of the 20th century. That's a paradox because today's planner has an arsenal of technological tools—from lighting to bridging and tunneling to materials for buildings—which urbanists even a hundred years ago could not begin to imagine: we have more resources to use than in the past, but resources we don't use very creatively.

This paradox can be traced to the over-determination both of the city's visual forms and its social functions. The technologies which make possible experiment have been subordinated to a regime of power which wants order and control. A classic example is Corbusier's "Plan Voisin" in the mid 1920's for Paris. The architect conceived of replacing a large swath of the historic centre of Paris with uniform, X shaped buildings; public life on the ground plane of the street would be eliminated; the use of all buildings would be coordinated by a single master plan. Not only is Corbusier's architecture a kind of industrial manufacture of buildings. He has tried in the "Plan Voisin" to destroy just that element which, as we will see, creates open-ness in a city. He got rid of life on the ground plane; instead, people live and work in isolation, higher up.[5]

Jacobs highlighted tactics, still relevant today, for making better cities through interventions such as pedestrian-oriented development, preservation of historic architecture, housing subsidies to ensure affordability, and strategies for ensuring economic viability. Jacobs's work served as a precursor to more recent movements such as sustainable cities and smart urbanism and, in part, contributed to the emergence of placemaking as not just a buzzword but a driving factor in modern planning activities.

More recently, the Project for Public Spaces (PPS) released a framework for great placemaking. This comprehensive approach, endorsed by the World Bank, identified six key aspects of placemaking: creates improved accessibility, builds and supports the local economy, supports social interaction, promotes health, nurtures and defines sense of community, and promotes a sense of comfort. The PPS has been very active in placemaking projects focused on Detroit's urban regeneration process. In partnership with Quicken Loans' founder Dan Gilbert, the PPS developed a placemaking strategy for downtown Detroit. Rock Ventures is the parent company for Quicken Loans that has also invested significantly in Detroit area real estate and related rebuilding projects. Clearly, Gilbert is embracing his role as not only a successful entrepreneur but also a civic innovator in Detroit's placemaking efforts.

At an event hosted by Dan Gilbert of Rock Ventures LLC, downtown Detroit became the Rust Belt comeback kid to watch. Gilbert, who moved thousands of employees downtown from his company Quicken Loans' former headquarters in the suburbs, has bought more than a dozen downtown properties in recent years and is deeply invested in the revitalization of the district. He is a new kind of visionary who understands the fundamental value of great places, and the need to work with his fellow citizens to shape the city's future together, rather than imposing a singular vision from the top down. The movement that he has built is about turning everything in Detroit upside down and reorienting the role of each player, from pedestrian to CEO, to maximize their contribution to the shared experience of the city.[6]

MIT's Department of Urban Studies and Planning (DUSP) recently highlighted the role of placemaking in building communities and supporting local economic development. They define placemaking as "the deliberate shaping of an environment to facilitate social interaction, create high-quality public space, and improve a community's quality of life."[7] They go on to note that placemaking provides opportunities "for people to collaborate, deliberate, disagree, and act." Places are made through multiple interactions among people through divergent and creative processes. Placemaking is not some grand master plan or achieved through a top-down command-and-control approach from local government. The idea of building community by means of placemaking has spread to all corners of the world. In Chile, for example, the Argentine technology entrepreneur Wenceslao Casares (who famously sold Patagon.com to Santander Bank right before the dot-com bubble burst) recently bought and refurbished a 1900s castle called "Las Majadas," to create what he calls "the conversations (epi)center" of Latin America. The purpose, as they state, is to build a factory of human relations that enables dialogue and ideas, which will subsequently contribute to creating a better Chile and Latin America.

I am biased, but I believe we can learn a lot from European cities regarding placemaking. Europeans were experts at placemaking long before we ever created the term. I have had the opportunity to live in Copenhagen, Madrid, and now Barcelona and have traveled to dozens of cities in Europe. What most of them seem to have in common is serious walkability, fantastic preserved architecture along with top-notch public transit systems. European cities were not, like many U.S. cities, designed for the car, but rather for people, in large part because European cities were built before Edwin Drake created the first commercial oil-drilling operation in the 1800s and well before Henry Ford introduced the Model T. European cities have generally done better at ensuring animated streets and retain many central plazas and terraces allowing for lots of social interaction. This inherent advantage Europe, which evolved frequently at a grassroots level over centuries, has will be discussed in the final chapter when I reflect on the future of urbanpreneurship in cities around the globe.

Of course, there are always outliers, and Singapore may be the best example of a city (city-state in the case of Singapore) that did utilize a top-down approach and managed to achieve impressive outcomes. Having recently visited both Singapore and Medellín, below I explore Singapore's top-down approach to placemaking and economic development and to juxtapose it with that of Medellín's bottom-up strategy.

## SINGAPORE AND MEDELLÍN: A TALE OF TWO DIFFERENT APPROACHES TO PLACEMAKING

By the late 1960s, Singapore had gained its independence from British rule, and emerged from a brief stint in a federation with Malaysia. It was a city-state with few natural resources, low productivity, and minimum economic development.

From the 1960s through the 1990s, Medellín, Colombia, was a haven for drug trafficking, resulting in one of the highest murder rates in the world. Economic development was stunted and the city in general suffered from a lack of infrastructure, basic services, and of course safe community spaces.

For different reasons, therefore, both Singapore and Medellín were poor and, from the outside, had little prospect of escaping their plights. Yet government leaders had different visions for their respective futures.

In Singapore, the government requested assistance from the United Nations to help them devise a decidedly top-down economic strategy for emerging out of the poverty. Through a concerted effort over a few decades, Singapore managed to invest in infrastructure and education resulting in the attraction of significant foreign investment. In recent years, Singapore has emerged as one of the most important hubs for multinational corporations in the Asia Pacific region. The key strategies for Singapore's transformation have been: (1) the government's strategic role, (2) mobilization of its human capital, and (3) continuous development of infrastructure.

I was fortunate enough to visit Singapore in 2012. The city-state is now a high-tech hub with world-class facilities and infrastructure. Singapore has invested in smart solutions to facilitate clean urban transport and to discourage personal vehicle use through a variable automated tolling system and very high taxes for acquiring the rights to vehicle ownership. It has an excellent park system and has also invested heavily in harvesting rainwater as part of a clear strategy to remove dependence on imported drinking water.

Despite all of this success, Singapore has significant challenges remaining. Tensions among lower-income classes have risen in recent years. The Gini coefficient, a measure of income inequality where 0 is the lowest inequality and 1 is the highest, was .463 for Singapore in 2013. To put this in perspective, Denmark's national Gini Index is .230.

The culture and governmental policies in Singapore are oriented toward multinationals. Although Singapore scores relatively highly on Richard Florida's Global Cities Index, the tolerance for entrepreneurial failure is low in Singapore as is the perceived desirability of entrepreneurship as a career path. In Singapore only 50.9 percent of the population considers entrepreneurship a good career choice and 39.7 percent of citizens have a fear of failure, according to the 2013 Global Entrepreneurship Monitor (GEM).[8]

Although the transformation of Medellín began with an entirely different process than that of Singapore, the results have been equally impressive. In the 1990s, the Medellín Academy began to push for a new city vision, which started by focusing on the poor communities on the periphery of the city. They brought their ideas to the city's poorest residents and began to co-evolve solutions for transportation, access to schools, work, and health care.

The former mayor of Medellín, Sergio Fajardo (2003–2007), embarked on a mission to "Close the door to crime and open the door to opportunity." While Singapore's transformation was largely top-down and government controlled, Medellín's was more organic, with a significant focus on bottom-up and citizen engagement.

Having visited Medellín in 2011, I must admit I left just as impressed with it as I would later be with Singapore. Both Medellín and Singapore are true success stories on a global scale. Yet, there is something under the surface that feels very different when experiencing both cities and when speaking with leaders and locals.

I believe some of it has to do with an entrepreneurial spirit. In Colombia, nearly 91 percent of citizens consider entrepreneurship a good career choice and 31.8 percent have a fear of failure according to the 2013 Global Entrepreneurship Monitor. I don't have the data, but I do know from spending a lot of time in Colombia, and meeting entrepreneurs from Medellín, that Medellín is actually considered the home of the creative and entrepreneurial communities in Colombia. Indeed, Medellín hosts one of the most relevant city programs in the region. Cultura E (Entrepreneurship Culture) and Parque E (Entrepreneurship Park) are two interconnected initiatives developed by the city between 2004 and 2006 with the aim of fostering entrepreneurial activities in the region and also permeating the Colombian culture with entrepreneurial principles. Of course, not all the "entrepreneurs" from Medellín have been benevolent—such as the infamous Pablo Escobar. Yet even Escobar initiated numerous civic projects, albeit not with altruistic intentions.

The top-down nature of Singapore's approach makes open innovation and civic entrepreneurship more challenging. Not to say it could never happen, but, for example, one expects civic crowdfunding and hackathons to be less likely in Singapore than in Medellín. Bottom-up collaboration, civic engagement and dialogue, and grassroots innovation are less likely to emerge under a command-and-control approach.

Medellín has a recent history of engaging its citizens in its transformation. It has a culture more supportive of entrepreneurship (and failure) than Singapore's. And it has begun to address head-on the challenges and opportunities of true social inclusion in ways that I believe suggest

Medellín is a model not just for Colombia or Latin America but perhaps for cities around the world to consider.

The Medellín Declaration, signed at the World Urban Forum in 2014, reinforces their commitment, and leadership, in ensuring that smart cities are also equitable cities.

Finding that right balance between supporting a creative and civic-minded entrepreneurial economy while bringing up the quality of life for all citizens is not an easy task. But we may find part of the answer by looking to Medellín for inspiration.

## THE CHANGING ROLE OF LOCAL CITIZENS

The Urbanpreneur Spiral model suggests that collaboration, urbanization, and democratization of innovation are contributing to a rise in urbanpreneurship. Combining the spiral model with the sense of place, we can see a rapidly changing role for local residents in their cities. Decades ago, and still to this day in some jurisdictions, citizens were presumed to be *passive recipients* of local laws, regulations, and welfare provision. In the 1980s some scholars and governments began exploring a shift of some local governments from treating citizens as passive recipients to treating them as *customers*. For example, a 1991 article in *Public Money & Management*, entitled "Citizens as Consumers: Marketing and Public Sector Management," documented the shift in applying marketing in communicating with and convincing citizens to embrace public policy, recycle more, or obey nonsmoking laws. This evolving relationship of treating citizens as customers still presumes a one-way relationship where the local government makes all the decisions but takes one more step in trying to make their citizen customers happy. Occasionally, the citizens as customers would also extend to engaging citizens to understand more about their needs and concerns, in hopes to better inform policy. This could also be referred to as *citizen engagement*.

One step beyond citizen engagement, which is widely used, is *citizen participation*, whereby citizens are proactively incorporated into policy development and visioning processes. In 2011, Vancouver's mayor, Gregor Robertson, led a citizen participation initiative aimed at developing a new vision for the city. After consultation with about 30,000 residents through a range of online and offline forums, residents committed to an aggressive plan to try to become the greenest city on the planet by 2020. While they may not reach their stretch goal, the effort to encourage the participation of so many residents in a new vision for the city was quite impressive.

Recently, a city in northern England went through a similar, yet more ludic process. In answering the questions, how can urban design improve the environment and what makes somewhere a good place to live?, the University of Newcastle and the city council created something called "The Great North Build." This initiative sought to involve the public in the construction of a giant Lego town to explore some of the major challenges that impact on people's everyday lives. The aim was to collectively build a mini-Newcastle, which took shape over the course of weeks, and the final form was determined by the public working with university researchers. The initiative was led by Newcastle's Institute for Social Renewal and the Newcastle City Council, but everyone was invited to participate:

From youngsters experimenting with chunky Duplo houses, to expert architects and city planners, everybody is invited to tackle the big questions. As the Lego town grows, micro-CCTV cameras will capture its development, and visitors can even expect to be challenged by unexpected real-life planning scenarios such as accommodating growing businesses or coping with flooding.[9]

One last step in this transformation in the relationship between city and citizen is *citizen co-creation*. Rather than considering the city to be the sole purveyor of welfare and quality of life, there is a growing interest from cities and concerned citizens to take a more active role in improving where they live. I consider this to be directly tied to how well the city has achieved placemaking as the more a citizen feels a sense of place, the more committed she will be to making her city better. Below I'll revisit civic hackers within the context of the first type of civic entrepreneur Pablo and I discovered through a series of interviews over the past few years.

## THREE TYPES OF CIVIC ENTREPRENEURS

Pablo and I worked on two recent research papers seeking to understand the emergence of civic entrepreneurs. In the course of this work we examined approximately 100 cases through interviews and secondary research in the civic innovation and entrepreneurship space. These were leaders within local government, individuals leading civic innovation incubators and accelerators, and civic entrepreneurs themselves. One of the many conversations that led to insights for me was one I had with Nigel Jacobs, the cofounder of Boston's New Urban Mechanics. I asked him to distinguish the difference between civic entrepreneurs and the more common term, *social entrepreneurs*. Nigel said that for him the difference between social entrepreneurs and civic entrepreneurs is that social entrepreneurs are generally trying to replace a void left by inefficient or ineffective government programs and institutions whereas civic entrepreneurs aim to address gaps in provision of services in communities via a collaboration with government. In other words, social entrepreneurs frequently seek to overcome the failures of the welfare state by replacing government services, whereas civic entrepreneurs look for opportunities to improve quality of life for target residents or visitors through collaborative business models with local governments.

I found Nigel's comparison quite informative personally, and Pablo and I leveraged this insight as we began to develop a model of civic entrepreneurship in our research projects. In one of those projects we sought to develop a strong theoretical model[10] for what makes civic entrepreneurship unique. In that model we realized that civic entrepreneurs are trying to solve gaps left by the market or government (i.e., market goods gap or public goods gap), that civic entrepreneurs are strongly embedded into both their social networks and the territory (i.e., embedded in place), and that they generally opt for collaborative business models among governments, citizens, and/or the private sector. Our second project on civic entrepreneurship specifically sought to uncover the collaborative approaches to business model development for civic entrepreneurs (Figure 3.1).

**Figure 3.1 Public-Private-People-Partnerships (4P) Civic Entrepreneur Model[11]**

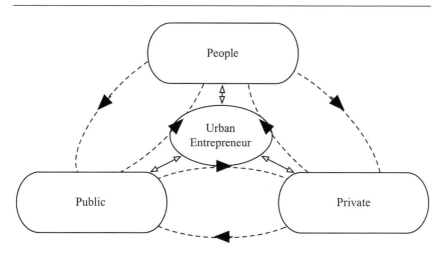

One of our theoretical model's variables relates to the way civic entrepreneurs are embedded in place. That is, civic entrepreneurs are prone to be inspired to improve the quality of life for their fellow citizens within different geographic boundaries. This is of course consistent with Jacobs's and other urbanists' ongoing work in placemaking described above. In our research we discovered three types of civic entrepreneurs: neighborhood based, city based, and global/platform based.

### Neighborhood-Based Civic Entrepreneurs (Civic Hackers)

Perhaps one of the most recognizable neighborhood-based civic entrepreneurs is Majora Carter. Born and raised in South Bronx, a tough part of New York City, Carter became a community organizer at a young age. In 2001, Carter founded a nonprofit group called Sustainable South Bronx to fight for environmental justice for the largely minority neighborhood. One of her first projects involved organizing the community to convince the city to resist the creation of a waste transition station in the neighborhood. Her campaign was successful. From the beginning Carter recognized the potential to use a combination of education and social enterprise to help build up the South Bronx neighborhood and to fight for environmental rights for the community. In recognition of Carter's ambitious and inspiring work with Sustainable South Bronx, the group was awarded a 500,000 (USD) award from the MacArthur Foundation, who glowingly described Carter's efforts this way:

Majora Carter, of the South Bronx, is determined to make her community more livable, greener, and healthier than it is today. The founder and director of Sustainable South Bronx (SSB), Carter is a relentless and charismatic urban strategist who seeks to address the disproportionate environmental and public health burdens experienced by residents of the South Bronx. Working in partnership with local government, businesses, and neighborhood organizations, she creates new opportunities for transportation, fitness and recreation, nutrition, and economic development.[12]

Neighborhood-level venturing involves, most of the time, one-off projects, embedded in what we call the "smallest significant socio-spatial scale." These projects are mostly associated with civil society collaborations and oftentimes dissolve after the completion of the project. In our research, we found that a majority of neighborhood-based civic ventures are not built with the intention of scaling, although in some cases the projects are replicated in other neighborhoods and copied by other civic entrepreneurs in other neighborhoods around the world. In Carter's case, she leveraged the notoriety obtained from her work with Sustainable South Bronx into a thriving national consultancy, Majora Carter Group. Ironically, in her new role she has upset some local community members due to a perception she has become too collaborative with the private sector, particularly in being a paid consultant to support the entry of a large grocery store into the community.[13]

### Civic Hacker Movement

It is this idea of citizen co-creation that has spawned a new wave of civic entrepreneurs who aspire to leverage entrepreneurial action to improve their communities. Nesta, the innovation agency in the UK, has been exploring this domain for some time now. By 2007, they were examining whether communities across the UK could take responsibility for their own carbon emissions. The Big Green Challenge, which was designed to encourage and support community-led responses to climate change, was a success with 350 neighborhoods coming forward generating a wide range of imaginative and practical ideas. Following the Big Green Challenge, Nesta launched other challenges aimed at fostering grassroots innovation. Community-led innovation partially responds to the capacities of communities to actually tackle their problems efficiently, and partially to the need to further involve the community in supporting the welfare state. Political drivers are still under debate, but there is a case to be made here around the power of communities in bringing about disruptive innovation.

The civic hacker movement has emerged as a grassroots model for citizen activism focused on reinforcing or building placemaking one neighborhood at a time. The civic hacker concept is a type of citizen cocreation, whereby neighborhood residents leverage their collective skills to reimagine their neighborhood and then take proactive steps, sometimes in collaboration with local governments, to make their vision a reality. Hackablecity.org has even developed a toolkit for civic hackers, which emerged from work done in Eixample, a historic neighborhood of Barcelona. The idea of hackable cities seems to be gaining some legitimacy globally. For example, in June 2015, a workshop entitled "Hackable Cities: From Subversive City Making to Systemic Change" was hosted by the University of Limerick in Ireland.

### City-Based Civic Entrepreneurs

Cities are essentially interconnected sets of neighborhoods, some with more commercial or industrial activity, some with more residential activity, and some with a mixture of uses. Since the scale and complexity to

implement innovation at the city level is sufficient to warrant the formation of an ongoing business, we have seen in our research that the majority of the entrepreneurship occurring at the city scale will likely take the
form of a city-based venture. Their development involve collaborations
with civil society and public institutions, including local city government
or regional and national government agencies.

In the past few years I have had the pleasure to visit Vienna, Austria, to
speak about smart cities with different city agencies and the long-term
mayor, Michael Haupl. Vienna is one of several leading cities to have a
proactive smart cities agenda. As part of this agenda, which includes an
ambitious roadmap to 2050, the city has created an agency responsible
for implementing smart city initiatives in collaboration with citizens
and the private sector. Dominic Weiss and Lukas Stockinger of Vienna
Austria's smart city agency, Tina Vienna, gave me a volume containing
more than 100 active smart cities projects in the city. One of those projects, Solar Citizen, particularly caught my attention as it illustrates the
city-level civic venturing. The Citizen Solar Power Plant is a collaborative project from Wien Energy and the city of Vienna. In a form of civic
crowdfunding, Citizen Solar enables local residents to micro-invest in
local renewable energy. Citizens can invest as little as 475 euros to own
a half of one solar panel or invest 950 euros to own one or more panels.
The Citizen Solar Power Plant aims to support the city's goal of obtaining
50 percent of its energy from renewable sources by 2030 while engaging
local residents as co-owners of the project. I would consider this to be a
corporate civic venture because it has been facilitated by a long-term
business model initiated by the local energy company, Wien Energy,
and been conducted in collaboration with the Vienna city government
and citizen investors.

## Global/Platform-Based Entrepreneurs

The final type of civic entrepreneur we discovered in our research is the
global/platform-based entrepreneur. This type of entrepreneur is concerned with city challenges but on a global scale. Global civic entrepreneurs frequently trying to find a scalable business model leveraging
platform-based business models. We consider platform-based urban ventures to be those that primarily leverage information and communications technologies (ICTs) enabling connections between two-sided
markets, such as the connection between citizens or local government
authorities and urban entrepreneurs. Platform entrepreneurs gain relevance as cities around the world build stronger links with other cities

beyond national boundaries, since they are able to replicate or scale the same or similar solutions in cities within a region or across the globe.

In this chapter, I have already introduced one such entrepreneur, Sascha Haselmayer, who was included in our interview process. His story is interesting because he started as neighborhood- and city-based civic entrepreneur and then pivoted with his cofounder to become a global civic entrepreneur. Sascha's path to a global civic entrepreneur is worth exploring more. The following description is based on an interview I conducted with Sascha in July 2013.

Sascha, originally from Germany, decided to study architecture at the Architectural Association School of Architecture (yes, you read that right). He conducted a field project in Soweto in 1993–1994 to work in a township with high levels of gang violence, unemployment, and pollution. He was studying how urban planning could be done in this complicated context. Not done with dangerous and challenging assignments, Haselmayer then went to Caracas for a year to develop a prototype for ensuring low-income residents' access to vote in presidential elections. This experience proved to Sascha that a combination of legal, economic, and urban mechanisms can be combined and scaled within a country.

After graduation, Sascha joined a private finance contracting company to understand how public services could be financed. He recognized that there were real differences between traditional public-private partnerships (3P models) and true collaboration involving local governments and the private sector. He felt there was a real need to move past the contractor mentality, which is still quite pervasive today in 3P projects and shift toward incentives for investment in trying to find win-win outcomes that benefit all parties including, of course, citizens.

In 2001, Sascha started a consultancy, Interlace, with a goal toward building knowledge-based communities. After a breakup with some of his original cofounders, Jakob Rasmussen joined and helped grow Interlace Invent through 2010 as a consultancy. The pair also launched Living Labs Global (LLG) to explore how cities can become living innovation laboratories through attracting a multi-stakeholder perspective to city projects and treating the city and its infrastructure as a test-bed for new technologies. LLG was succeeding as a consultancy, but Sascha was concerned they were stuck at the city-scale form of civic venturing, and he was really interested in finding a way to get to a more scalable, platform model. Sascha and Jakob then decided to pivot the company from a consultancy to a platform business using technology as a way to connect cities in search of new technologies and small and large providers of technology around the globe. Thus, Citymart was born. After plenty of early

Table 3.1 Place-based Civic Entrepreneurs, adapted from "The Making of the Urban Entrepreneur," *California Management Review,* 2016.

| Action/place | Neighborhood | City | Multi-City |
|---|---|---|---|
| Strategy | Project-based strategy | New venture-based strategy | Platform-based strategy |
| Type of collaboration | Temporary task force—one-off effort | Coalition-intermittent coordination | Alliance-regular coordination |
| Business model | Emerging initiatives | Hybrid business modeling | Collaborative partnerships—global movement |
| Growth strategy | Project replication | Venture scaling-up | Network expansion |
| Primary funding strategy | Membership, donations, or crowdfunding | Impact investing | International-national agencies |
| Organizational form | NGO—community interest company | Hybrid organization | Network structure |
| Primary policy instrument | Neighborhood-oriented contests | Venture incubation or acceleration | Interagencies city innovation hubs |

frustrations and challenges from investors who were afraid of their dependence on revenues from local governments, they were able to close a $1 million round from a Finnish investment firm, Plastillin, at the end of 2013.

Interestingly, a common thread Pablo and I discovered in virtually all of our interviews with civic entrepreneurs is that Sascha and his partners do not aspire to an exit the way many technology-based entrepreneurs do. Exits are where founders of start-ups either take their start-up public (an initial public offering) or sell their company to an acquirer. Sascha is committed to making Citymart a profitable company, but he believes maintaining independence is critical so they can serve as an impartial mediator of their two-sided market. Table 3.1, adapted from my forthcoming paper with Pablo Muñoz in the *California Management Review*, provides a summary of the neighborhood-, city-, and platform-based civic entrepreneurs we have discovered.

## THE EMERGENCE OF CIVIC TECH

The Knight Foundation was founded in Ohio in 1950 to provide support for a range of educational, journalistic, and community initiatives locally and throughout the United States. In the 1990s the foundation launched the Community Foundations Initiative to support local community resilience and innovation in 26 U.S. cities. Since then, the Knight Foundation has become an important player in supporting the civic entrepreneurship revolution, offering annual awards to the best emerging civic tech innovators. In March 2015, the Knight Foundation announced the 32 winners of the first Knight Cities Challenge. The winners were selected from 7,000 applications and 126 finalists. The largest prize (650,000 USD) was offered to "ArtHouse: A Social Kitchen" in Gary, Indiana, which aspires to incubate new restaurant and food concepts in the city. The smallest award (20,000 USD) went to a neighborhood project in Philadelphia, proposed by the Central Roxborough Civic Association, to support neighborhood regeneration projects by introducing a new zoning called "Neighborhood Conservation Overlay." All of the winning projects would likely fall within a broad conceptualization of civic entrepreneurship, whether they were proposed by a citizen, a startup, or a nonprofit organization.

## CIVIC TECH IN ACTION

Many of the civic entrepreneurs discussed above and in our interviews leverage technology to deliver value. Of course there are many examples of non-tech or low-tech civic entrepreneurs, usually found at the neighborhood level such as Repair Cafes or community edibles gardens. In parallel with the emergence of civic entrepreneurs has been an explosion in growth of the civic tech space. Civic tech is a subset of government technology focused specifically on supporting the interface between governments and citizens, as opposed to technology used by governments for internal purposes. In early 2015, the research consultancy IDC reported that $6.4 billion would be spent on civic tech by the end of that same year.

I consider the civic tech space to be somewhat of a hybrid between the urban tech entrepreneurs discussed in the previous chapter and the civic entrepreneurs in this one. Whereas the research Pablo and I have developed on civic entrepreneurs suggests that civic entrepreneurs are focused on improving quality of life of local citizens and usually part of the local fabric of the city (except for global, platform-based civic entrepreneurs), and are frequently driven by social and/or sustainable objectives, much of the civic tech arena is led by multinational corporations and profit-driven entrepreneurs. However, there is quite a bit of gray area here in that the civic tech arena also has many founders driven by the same values we discovered are common among civic entrepreneurs. Thus, while some civic entrepreneurs use technology and some civic tech entrepreneurs could be classified as civic entrepreneurs, they are not, in my opinion, the same, nor are they mutually exclusive.

Take, for example, the case of Siemens, the multinational technology company based in Berlin, reorganization, at the end of 2011. Siemens announced it was reorganizing, in part to more directly go after opportunities in the cities market. The new organization was named Infrastructure & Cities. While Siemens is a strong global company with a great reputation for innovation, it is not what I would consider a classical example of a civic entrepreneurial firm. Yet their work in cities could contribute to improved efficiencies and, in the case of civic tech, could also result in improved quality of life. Thus, the gray area.

Driven in part by citizens' increasing demands to engage with local governments via mobile and Web services, the civic tech arena is being used for citizen participation, data access, visualization, and even online and mobile voting tools. Many of you will be familiar with the smart phone application Waze. Waze was founded in 2008 by Israeli entrepreneurs, with the goal of creating a crowdsourced GPS navigation tool that relies on the community to update information regarding traffic congestion, accidents, and detours and even to avoid police roadblocks. The application quickly grew in user base, supported by early funding from U.S. venture capital funding, and expanded its service in cities around the globe. In 2013, Google acquired Waze for 1.1 billion (USD). Cities began to recognize the value of the data created by the Wazer user community, and in 2014, Waze announced the launch of the Connected Citizens program, which will allow Waze and participating cities to collaborate on data sharing from sensors, real-time traffic information, and other navigation information. The first 10 cities to join the program included Barcelona, Boston, Los Angeles, Rio de Janeiro, San Jose (Costa Rica), and Tel Aviv. Waze is a classic example of how civic tech companies are enabling cities to improve service delivery while also engaging citizens as collaborators in content generation.

## CIVIC ENTREPRENEURSHIP AND OPEN INNOVATION

Part of the driving force behind the rise of urbanpreneurship has been the democratization of innovation and technology. One outcome of the democratization process has been the growth in open innovation models whereby organizations embrace stakeholders as participants in the innovation process. Open innovation, first introduced by Henry Chesbrough, has become a common practice by corporations in the twenty-first century. But open innovation has come to cities too. And it poses the potential to stimulate all kinds of opportunities for civic entrepreneurs. Sascha Haselmayer, who cofounded Citymart.com, which is based in Barcelona and Copenhagen, provides a good example of such a civic-minded entrepreneur thinking on a large scale. Citymart seeks to be an intermediator between civic innovators and cities in search of new solutions. Citymart provides a validation service for civic technology providers whereby Citymart obtains data from both the tech company and the cities where the provider purports to have tested their solutions. The validation service enhances the visibility of the provider on Citymart's platform while providing increased confidence from global cities in the claims of the provider.

But more interesting than that basic validation from Citymart is their recent foray into hosting open innovation competitions for cities. Their first such project was with the city of Barcelona, which launched a program called the BCN Open Challenge. Local and national governments are famous for their bureaucratic approaches to procurement, which lead to time-consuming and expensive proposals and barriers to entry into government contracts too high for start-ups and citizens with good ideas. The goal of Citymart's new service, piloted by Barcelona, is to make local government contracts more accessible to start-ups and innovators of all sizes by streamlining the procurement process. But besides eliminating traditional procurement barriers, the process embraces open innovation by only identifying the problems in need of solutions as opposed to specifying the desired features of the solution.

Instead of predetermining the specifications of desired solutions, the Ayuntamiento de Barcelona identified six challenges and posted these challenges in Catalan, Spanish, and English on a global ideas platform for cities (Citymart.com). Barcelona received 119 proposals from citizens and companies around the globe and is in the process of contracting the winners to implement their innovative proposals.

Open civic innovation goes beyond procurement, however. For example one of the biggest triggers for civic entrepreneurs in recent years has been the trend toward transparency and open data. Cities are choosing to open up hundreds, and in some cases thousands, of databases to allow citizens and entrepreneurs permitting the development of applications for citizens and residents. Not only are cities opening up previously closed data sets, but new data sets are being generated through the use of new technologies. Sensor technology to measure everything from weather, traffic congestion, and air contamination is being implemented in cities around the globe. Additionally, real-time data are being generated by other ICT devices in what many refer to as the Internet of Things

(IoT), such as bluetooth technology in vehicles and smartphone use. All of these data are also being opened to support new innovative solutions aimed at improving quality of life in cities. IoT is big business and will lead to major innovations and entrepreneurial and corporate successes. The global consultancy Accenture, for example, released a report in early 2015 projecting that the global IoT sector will be worth $14 trillion by 2030.[14] More insights on what cities are or could be doing to promote civic and other forms of urban entrepreneurship will be discussed in Chapter 6.

## CONCLUSION

In this chapter I presented several underlying factors such as the evolution of cities, economics of cities, and placemaking to help explain the emergence of the civic entrepreneurship space in cities around the globe. I presented results of my research with Pablo Muñoz on different types of civic entrepreneurs (neighborhood, city, and platform) and presented several examples and insights emerging from our interviews of actors in the civic entrepreneurship ecosystem around the globe. While civic entrepreneurs are similar to other forms of entrepreneurship, such as sustainable entrepreneurship (e.g., Zeronauts from Steve Elkington) or social entrepreneurship (e.g., Blessed Unrest by Paul Hawken), they are also unique in their attachment to place and their desire to improve the lives of their neighbors and community through collaborative business models with local governments and other stakeholders.

After conducting more than a dozen interviews from leading actors in this arena, Pablo and I realized that civic entrepreneurship is seriously challenging the logic of formal market structures, forcing scholars, entrepreneurs, and policy makers alike to reframe their thinking around the interactions between place, individuals, institutions, and the innovative outcomes of civic-oriented enterprising behavior. Shortly after our first paper was written, we realized that the historic business paradigm is under stress. Civic entrepreneurs no longer identify markets as the single-most important playing field for their actions, nor profit maximization as the primary objective of business activity. New ventures, corporations, public institutions, and civil society recognize the need to transition from carbon-intensive economic activity to incorporating the true costs of social and environmental externalities into a new type of business modeling. With this, actors are starting to acknowledge that such a task cannot be achieved through single agency, but rather through collaborative, innovative, and place-sensitive action that creates solutions partially within and partially outside formal structures. We believe that this is the key mechanism that is putting pressure on the business-as-usual logic as never before. Extant rules of the game can handle sustainable and social entrepreneurship, but have proven incapable of handling the complexity involved in this emerging form of entrepreneurial action, which involves and requires interactions among numerous stakeholders and citizens, which utilize the city as a platform for open innovation experiments.

In the next chapter, I will discuss another form of entrepreneur emerging from the Urbanpreneur Spiral, that of the Indie Urbanpreneur.

# CHAPTER 4

## The Rise of the Indie Urbanpreneurship Space

As previously discussed, the great urban migration sets the scene for the emergence of new urban entrepreneurship spaces. The civic entrepreneurship space has enabled dialogue, collaboration, and multistakeholders interactions aimed at addressing city challenges. Yet, there is another type of urbanpreneur who is shaping, and being shaped by, cities. The independent, or indie, urbanpreneur is also a product of the converging trends of collaboration, urbanization, and democratization, which are enabling new, or arguably improved, forms of freelancing for urban residents. In this chapter I will present three forms of indie urbanpreneurs that are gaining traction and poised for growth in the coming years. These include "on-demand," "makers," and "digital" indie urbanpreneurs.

### INDEPENDENCE AND THE NEW "ENTREPRENEUR"

There has always been a percentage of the workforce who preferred to be a freelance specialist, picking up contracting projects as opposed to working in a corporation or starting a company. Even more so with the explosion of the Internet, which, by the mid-2000s, extended the long tail of markets enabling the emergence and survival of niche products and services. In 2006, the Government Accountability Office reported that 30 percent of the U.S. working-age population was employed in some sort of freelance or temporary role.[1] Yet, less than 10 years later, the figure had risen to 34 percent, representing 53 million freelancers in 2014.[2] According to Sara Horowitz, director of the Freelancers Union, "Freelancing is the new normal—and this survey shows that America's new workforce is big, crucial and here to stay." The Freelancers Union survey found that millennials make up a disproportionately higher percentage (38 percent) of freelancers than other age groups in the United States. Across the Atlantic, the European Forum of Independent Professionals (EFIP) was founded in 2010 to represent the 11 million independent professionals (iPros) with the European Union governing bodies. According to EFIP, the number of iPros in the EU grew 45 percent between 2004 and 2014. In 2014, EFIP launched the Freelancers Manifesto, which called for increased visibility for the sector including representation in official statistics (note EFIP claims iPros are the fastest growing component of the EU labor market), improved regulation to support iPros, and the creation of a special envoy to "champion the benefits of independent working."

The question becomes why does it appear millennials are embracing the freelance lifestyle more than previous generations? Of course, part of the answer is that it may not always be their choice. The younger generation, particularly after the Great Recession,[3] has had a harder time finding full-time paid employment as they have entered the workforce. Youth unemployment rates in Spain, for example, reached an astounding record high of 55 percent in 2013.[4] Also, with the downturn in the economy, companies have embraced the reduced costs associated with full-time employees and, instead, sought employees willing to settle for less employer commitment. A study by the National Employment Law Project found that the shift to temporary, contract work has saved employers 22 percent in payroll costs.[5]

However, I am convinced there are more factors driving millennials to consider alternative, freelance-style employment. In 2013, Genesis Research Associates conducted a study of 4,000 freelancers worldwide, half of which would be classified as millennials.[6] Here are some surprising numbers that emerged from the survey: 72 percent of those surveyed who are currently also in a traditional job and just moonlight on the side prefer to quit and become completely independent. These same moonlighters indicated that the freedom to work wherever they please (92 percent), whenever they like (87 percent), and on more interesting projects (67 percent) were among the biggest draws for becoming fully independent. Another interesting result was that 90 percent of the survey respondents consider being an entrepreneur a mindset and only 10 percent suggested that being an entrepreneur requires the formation of a new company. As scholars in the entrepreneurship arena, Pablo and I have observed that the growth in entrepreneurial freelancers is challenging existing paradigms in the field. I believe this mentality toward independence and entrepreneurship is going to continue to drive the growth of indie urbanpreneurs throughout the world.

## THE GROWING IMPORTANCE AND AVAILABILITY OF SOFT INFRASTRUCTURE IN CITIES

A forward thinking city knows that building attractive amenities is not enough to draw inhabitants. Citizens today seek a climate for ideas and exchange. . . . By fostering an environment of innovation and collaborative exchange, cities can engage both local and international audiences, and position themselves to attract active community members.[7]

Yet too many cities and their urban planners seem to be focused more on hard infrastructure, highways, buildings, and energy grids than on the soft infrastructure that underlies vibrant, creative cities. Charles Landry and his colleague recognized this challenge decades ago in their book *The Creative City*:

We need to enrich the "scientific" and quantitavist tradition with insights gained from more qualitative, human-oriented approaches (to creative city planning)—ranging from history and philosophy to religion and the arts. Planners find it easier to think in terms of expenditures on highways, car parks and physical redevelopment schemes rather than on soft infrastructures such as training initiatives for skills enhancement, the encouragement of a lively night-time economy, grants to voluntary organizations to develop social networks or social innovation and the decentralization of powers to build up local capacity and encouraging people to have a stake in the running of their neighborhoods.[8]

While Landry and Bianchini were right regarding the need for cities and urban planners to embrace bottom-up innovation and soft infrastructure, the past five years have seen some significant changes to the urban landscape related to the soft infrastructure that supports entrepreneurship in cities. Although all urbanpreneurs may benefit from them, I believe the indie urbanpreneur not only benefits more from soft infrastructure, but in some cases, newer soft infrastructure in cities actually give rise to some indie urbanpreneurs because without that infrastructure, they could not design, build, or distribute their innovations.

## URBAN ENTREPRENEURIAL ECOSYSTEMS

The World Bank study on urban tech innovation ecosystems discussed in Chapter 2 identified four categories of factors that have been found to promote the growth of entrepreneurial ecosystems in urban environments: human capital, physical assets, economic assets, and enabling environment, in other words, people, infrastructure, funding, and policy. Only one category, physical assets or infrastructure, reflects the tangible, physical infrastructure in a city that can give rise to vibrant ecosystems. The other three could be referred to as the "invisible infrastructure" of urban entrepreneurial ecosystems.

The World Bank report considers economic assets to include items such as the diversity and size of companies and industries, proximity to research universities and R&D facilities, the presence and maturity of creative and technology-based industries, and the presence of innovation-oriented investment firms. This category is consistent with most prior research on factors influencing the growth of local entrepreneurial ecosystems so it was no surprise to find it as a key factor in the World Bank's model.

The enabling environment focuses on government policy and programs and other underlying resources and institutions that can support the growth of entrepreneurial ecosystems. However, the other enabling conditions are potentially powerful for indie urbanpreneurs. The Brookings Institution's work on innovation districts suggests that the enabling environment for more vibrant urban entrepreneurial ecosystems consists of items such as coworking spaces and meetups, which I believe are powerful examples of the soft infrastructure that can not only facilitate positive collisions, or interactions, but may also give rise to indie urbanpreneurs.

## COWORKING

Frequently, indie urbanpreneurs gain access to coworking spaces instead of having permanent offices or working from home, to gain access to office resources and possible "collisions" with like-minded urbanpreneurs at a fraction of the cost of a formal office. It seems that these spaces are starting to replace the traditional entrepreneurship support infrastructure. In London, for example, a recent study identified 112 operating coworking spaces, compared to only 34 new ventures incubators and 16 business accelerators.[9] According to CoworkingSpain.es, Barcelona had 339 coworking spaces throughout the city as of October 2015. Coworking spaces are modern-day, open-office formats for shared use by individuals, instead of companies, engaged in creative, entrepreneurial, and other primarily independent activities. Coworking spaces usually have high-speed Internet connections, shared office resources like printers and meeting rooms, and frequently cafes too. Some spaces focus on specific industries or business approaches, such as Toronto's Centre for Social Innovation, which offers a variety of workspaces for socially charged projects, or Huckletree in London, which focuses only on new and emerging technologies. Most coworking spaces, however, are multipurpose cool spots for accelerating entrepreneurship in all its diverse forms. The explosion of coworking spaces is fairly recent; half of the ones identified in the London study were established only in the last two years.

Increasingly, coworking spaces are becoming hubs or major nodes of connections within the indie urbanpreneurship and broader entrepreneurial ecosystems in their communities. In the case of London, the majority of the coworking infrastructure is located in four inner London boroughs (Westminster, Camden, Islington, and Hackney), with a particular concentration in and around Tech City. A *Harvard Business Review* article reported results of a 2011 survey of more than 1,500 coworkers in 52 countries.[10] The results were quite telling. Seventy-five percent of respondents reported an increase in productivity since joining a coworking space, 80 percent experienced an increase in the size of their business network, and 86 percent reported a decrease in sense of isolation. Keep in mind, before coworking spaces emerged, many of these freelancers worked from home so these results suggest that coworking spaces can be powerful sources of inspiration for indie urbanpreneurs and facilitate collision density and innovation.

Sacramento, California, is one of the many cities around the globe experiencing a boom in demand for coworking facilities. Three of Sacramento's coworking facilities were rated among the top 25 in the United States. Some coworking spaces are part of a new breed of 3D labs, which offer access to equipment such as 3D printers to facilitate prototyping onsite with their shared facilities. This is the case for Hacker Lab, one of the top-rated facilities in Sacramento, which actively promotes interactions among coworkers in its facilities and also hosts several hacker events every year in hopes of facilitating collisions that result in new innovations. Sacramento's mayor Kevin Johnson expressed his perception of the growing importance of such coworking facilities in support of local innovation ecosystems:

Like the assembly line of past generations, co-working spaces will be the drivers of our new economy. In this new era, which I call Sacramento 3.0, where we are a hub of innovation, technology and entrepreneurship, we need to create more co-working spaces like Hacker Lab that will help foster an environment of entrepreneurs working in a community, where they can create, develop and share better ideas faster.[11]

Coworking is much larger than a North American and European phenomenon. Coworking spaces first emerged on the scene in 2005 with Small Business Labs estimating that there will be 12,000 coworking spaces in cities around the globe by 2018.[12] For example, coworking has taken off in Cape Town, South Africa, with support of the city as part of their efforts to support the growth of their already vibrant entrepreneurial ecosystem. While some of Cape Town's coworking spaces are targeted to early-stage tech start-ups, like Bandwidth Barn and Cape Town Garage, many others are dedicated to supporting a broader range of independent and creative workers. For example, Inner City Ideas Cartel considers itself the perfect working space for urban entrepreneurs and seeks to inspire, encourage, and enable our members by giving them the tools they need to create a daily work experience that brings them happiness, opportunity, increased income, and meaning.[13]

I have experienced the benefits of urban coworking spaces directly. In 2012 and early 2013, I was the director of the Center for Entrepreneurship at a private university about 30 minutes outside of Buenos Aires. One of my primary roles was to help grow the role of the university with the greater Buenos Aires entrepreneurial ecosystem. However, I found that the university's location in a northern suburb really detracted from my ability to integrate with the entrepreneurial community. So I decided to move to one of the key entrepreneurial neighborhoods of Buenos Aires, Palermo Soho, and work out of a coworking space (Urban Station) instead of my university office. The easy access to urbanpreneurs and other accelerators and entrepreneurial actors in the neighborhood was very helpful. It facilitated collisions with other entrepreneurs and other members of the ecosystem. It was also a much more enjoyable atmosphere to work in than a traditional boring, isolated university office.

## FROM SINGULAR COWORKING IN ONE CITY TO GLOBAL "WORKTATION" INDIE URBANPRENEURS

Urban Station is one of hundreds of coworking companies that have multiple locations not just in the city where they were founded (Buenos Aires), but in other cities in the region and the globe. One of the benefits of having multiple locations is that by being a member of one coworking facility in the network, urbanpreneurs can gain access to multiple locations when traveling for business or pleasure. This leads to another approach taken by some indie urbanpreneurs who hop from city to city when their independent business permits remote activity. The online magazine E27 summarized this form of "worktation" in a 2015 post:

With the rising trend of co-working, remote work, and "workation" retreats, entrepreneurial Millennials from around the world are quickly adopting the location-independent entrepreneurship lifestyle because of the prospect of reduced living costs, exciting new environments, and access to a network of other motivated and interesting creatives and entrepreneurs.

For example, Workaway, the travel agency for entrepreneurs, offers trips for 7–14 days around the world, including retreats in Italy, Spain, Morocco, Costa Rica, Tanzania, Kenya, and Russia; we hear they will be launching to Asia soon. First-time entrepreneurs intent on launching an online business see Southeast Asia as an ideal place because of the warm climates and extensive network of expatriates already living the region.[14]

I believe we are going to see a lot more of this in the coming years given the trends of collaboration and democratization discussed throughout this book. Because it is easier to do more with less, and because of the growth of the sharing economy, indie urbanpreneurs can leverage coworking spaces, but also temporary and shared housing through Airbnb and similar services, as well as tap into local (wherever they are traveling at the moment) and global service providers for on-demand project support. Furthermore, the possibility to see the world, while working out of fun new cities and meeting new people, will likely appeal to many millennials. Actually, as I write this, as a generation Xer, I am feeling envy and a longing to try out that lifestyle. Of course, it is much easier for single people or empty nesters. I recently uncovered this story in *New York* magazine about another woman worthy of envy, who has seen the potential of this multicity indie urbanpreneur lifestyle:

For the past three years, Martin-Austin has been spending several months a year in Berlin, working remotely for her design clients in New York and hanging out. Like a growing number of Americans, she works from her laptop and can easily telecommute. "I can just Skype into meetings," Martin-Austin says, "and I use Google Wallet to transfer money." Berlin's cheap enough to begin with, and because she gets paid from New York, where salaries are higher, her money goes a lot further than it would back home. "Being broke in Berlin is more fun because everyone in Berlin is broke," she says.[15]

## OPPORTUNITIES FOR COLLISIONS—MEETUPS

One of the benefits of coworking for indie urbanpreneurs is the networking that occurs among other creative, entrepreneurial members. Some coworking facilities host their own social events, usually around entrepreneurial themes to encourage interaction among members and others from the local entrepreneurial community. Relatedly, in cities around the globe, proactive community members develop interest groups around specific themes or topics related to a range of topics. Meetups and informal collisions that occur in cities are key factors in the success of the indie urbanpreneur. While some entrepreneurs can, for example, code by themselves in their home, most indie urbanpreneurs (even coders) benefit from regular social interaction with a diverse amount of individuals in their community.

The Bostonian designer community is particularly active in this respect, and the Dribbble platform has been responding to the demand. Instead of just allowing designers to sell their products online, Dribbble is open for designers, illustrators, and other creative individuals to share small screenshots that show their work, process, and current projects. Since Dribbble is a place to show and tell, promote, discover, and explore design, the online platform went offline to develop Dribbble Meetups, which offer designers the chance to socialize, talk, and foster their local design communities. Meetups are self-organized events, supported by Dribbble, that gather designers around the world on a weekly basis. I just went online and found Dribbble Meetups in a one-week period in places such as Penang (Malaysia), Minsk (Belarus), Łódź (Poland), Athens (Greece), London (United Kingdom), Miami, Montreal, Chicago, Austin, Baton Rouge, Los Angeles, and Cebu City in the Philippines. The themes for these meetups range from highly sophisticated Web platform designs to skills swap parties for Halloween.

Meetup.com is the largest online platform for posting invites to local meetups. I wrote this chapter while I was still living in Santiago, Chile. On this day, Sunday, April 5, 2015, there are 129 meetup groups with events in the next month in Santiago alone. There are literally dozens of meetups directly related to the startup community, such as Asao de Startup, which focuses on building networks for the start-up community with more than 1,700 members; Mujeres Emprendedoras de Chile ("female Chilean entrepreneurs") with 213 members; Santiago Startup Founder 101 with 362 members; EmprendoVerder ("green entrepreneurship") with 1,800 members; and Startup Grind Santiago with 340 members, among many others. But there are also many other meetups that have the potential to cross-pollinate the urbanpreneurs from coding-specific meetups (e.g., Women who code Santiago with 257 coders), technology-focused meetups (e.g., New Tech Santiago with 432 members), hacker groups (e.g., Hacks/Hackers Chile with 798 members), and industry vertical groups (e.g., Health 2.0 Santiago with 192 members).

Of course, all of these "invisible infrastructure" elements identified by the World Bank contribute to what combine to form the networking assets. No matter how much technology we have that permits us to remain virtual and make thousands of "friends" on Facebook, LinkedIn, Twitter, and other social networks, the research is clear that thriving urban entrepreneurial ecosystems depend on the quality, diversity, and frequency of regular interactions and "collisions," which occur among current and future participants in the local ecosystem.

Within this world of freelance, independent entrepreneurs, I have identified three subtypes of the indie urbanpreneur. These include the on-demand urbanpreneur, the maker urbanpreneur, and the digital urbanpreneur.

## INDIE URBANPRENEURS: ON DEMAND

While much of this book has had a technology bias to the urban entrepreneurial revolution, the urbanpreneur has expanded well beyond such technology-focused service provision. Yet, in many cases, even when the urbanpreneur is not developing a technology solution, they are increasingly benefiting from technology platforms that connect indie urbanpreneurs with short-term projects. The first subtype of indie urbanpreneur I will present is the "on-demand" indie urbanpreneur. The on-demand economy has emerged as one term; others include the "gig economy," to describe the growing use of platforms to connect individuals with short-term, just-in-time-type project opportunities. These opportunities run the gamut from high-tech and design to odd jobs around people's homes. Of course, the on-demand economy's most famous, or infamous, platform is Uber, which connects drivers of privately owned vehicles with those seeking rides. Uber has since expanded their business model and services in numerous other directions, such as UberEats, which facilitates home-food delivery.

## TWO-SIDED PLATFORMS FOR SHORT-TERM WORK

Increasingly, there are numerous platform ventures focused on connecting such indie urbanpreneurs to short-term projects from companies or other individuals. One of the most successful platform ventures for jobs is Elance. Recall my green mobile start-up, 3rdWhale.com. In an effort to keep costs low and develop a minimum viable product at the cheapest cost, we sought out mobile app developers via Elance.com. I had no personal expertise in programming of any kind, let alone for mobile apps. This was in 2009 when the App Stores like Apple's and Blackberry's were just beginning to offer access to third-party developers. Being cash strapped, and at the time running 3rdWhale out of a coworking facility at Simon Fraser

University in Vancouver, utilizing Elance was the most cost-effective and timely way to develop the first beta apps for the service I had envisioned.

Elance, based in Mountain View, California has raised about $100 million to scale its platform connecting independents and small service providers with customers around the globe seeking graphic design, programming, and related project support. oDesk was founded in San Francisco, California, in 2003, by two Greek entrepreneurs seeking to facilitate connections between independent professionals and companies seeking contractor support for their projects. At the end of 2013, Elance and oDesk merged to create Upwork, a powerful alliance of two of the largest platform providers in the temporary work arena. Upwork claims to represent more than 2 million businesses and 9.7 million freelancers from 180 countries generating close to $1 billion in work on an annual basis. The remote production of digital services for clients around the globe is not necessarily exclusive to the urbanpreneurship revolution because providers of remote programming and digital services can literally live anywhere in the world, and not necessarily in cities. Yet the emergence of platforms for connecting customers seeking short-term project work validated the market opportunity for platform providers and has led to the introduction of platforms that do in fact support the growth of on-demand indie urbanpreneurs.

TaskRabbit, for example, is part of the "on-demand economy" in urban settings. Leveraging the ubiquitous nature of smartphones and other information and communication technologies (ICTs), platform providers are able to connect providers of services with user demand in real time and often location based, such as the case with TaskRabbit. TaskRabbit connects providers of basic services (contractors) from gardening to roofing and anything in between with individuals seeking that service. TaskRabbit has exploded and now counts approximately 1.25 million users. Most individuals providing services via TaskRabbit have sought to use it as a source of supplemental income, while about 10 percent of TaskRabbit contractors used the platform as their sole source of income. Reflecting on the explosion of TaskRabbit, Joshua Brustein, from Bloomberg Business, says:

By moving from errands to real work, TaskRabbit is betting on a future where employment will seem much more like a series of small-scale agreements between businesses and labor than jobs in the traditional sense. Ten percent of the people who take jobs through the service do so full-time, earning as much as $60,000 a year before taxes.

Uber is another platform in the on-demand economy, which connects drivers of private vehicles with passengers seeking to go from point A to point B. Uber is not really part of the sharing economy because it is not about optimizing subutilized resources. Uber is essentially a virtual taxi fleet, without owning any of the vehicles. Because Uber's business model is a clear threat to taxi fleets, and because Uber has largely avoided the regulation associated with taxi operators, driver security screening, and taxes of taxi fleets, Uber has faced an uphill battle in gaining local government support for their operations. Despite their regulatory challenges, Uber has seen exponential growth since its launch in 2009. In July 2012 Uber had only a few thousand drivers in the United States and by January 2015, the number of active Uber drivers had reached more than 150,000.[16]

Many consider Uber's business model to be just the tip of the iceberg with respect to where the on-demand economy is going. Take for example this excerpt from a *New York Times* article in 2015:

But of all the ways that Uber could change the world, the most far-reaching may be found closest at hand: your office. Uber, and more broadly the app-driven labor market it represents, is at the center of what could be a sea change in work, and in how people think about their jobs. You may not be contemplating becoming an Uber driver any time soon, but the Uberization of work may soon be coming to your chosen profession.

Just as Uber is doing for taxis, new technologies have the potential to chop up a broad array of traditional jobs into discrete tasks that can be assigned to people just when they're needed, with wages set by a dynamic measurement of supply and demand, and every worker's performance constantly tracked, reviewed and subject to the sometimes harsh light of customer satisfaction. Uber and its ride-sharing competitors, including Lyft and Sidecar, are the boldest examples of this breed, which many in the tech industry see as a new kind of start-up—one whose primary mission is to efficiently allocate human beings and their possessions, rather than information.[17]

The on-demand economy has plenty of detractors. For example, in that same *New York Times* article, Dr. Robert Reich, a University of California-Berkeley economist, concluded after interviewing several on-demand workers:

I think it's nonsense, utter nonsense. This on-demand economy means a work life that is unpredictable, doesn't pay very well and is terribly insecure.

Reich was secretary of Labor in the Clinton administration, and his work focuses on labor, capitalism, and democracy and, in particular, on how changes in macro-conditions (trends, interest rates, etc.) affect jobs security, wages, and subsequently equality. Of course, from this point of view, the on-demand economy offers a near-to-zero security, but for certain there are people who value the flexibility, dynamism, or risks associated with on-demand labor. Some of them, I would guess, had no access to the formal economy before (i.e., job security and steady wages) and now they see in these platforms a way to offer their services, ranging from millennials constantly looking for new challenges to full-time moms, dads, or even seniors looking for flexible job opportunities. The on-demand economy is neither the recipe for eradicating inequality nor the source of it. Instead it is an alternative form of labor that simply adds more diversity to an already diversified economy.

Reich, many regulators, incumbent competitors, and others have vocally criticized the on-demand economy as it tends to drive down the value of work while offering few benefits of traditional full-time employment. Yet there are organizations seeking to use similar platforms to combat the lack of collective bargaining power of on-demand workers. One such platform for supporting collective action by on-demand workers is called Dynamo. It was developed by a Stanford research team and at the time of writing was only serving the needs of Mechanical Turk, an Amazon.com on-demand platform. I presume Dynamo, and other similar platforms to follow, will soon harness the power of the masses of on-demand contractors across different job platforms to demand better treatment, income, and benefits.

Regardless of the criticisms and their potential validity, I believe on-demand labor is here to stay and will likely represent a larger percentage of the global workforce in the coming years. An increasing amount of these workers will "choose" this as a full-time approach due to the flexibility, independence, variety, and lack of better full-time options. Increasingly this work, largely urban in nature, will also move upstream to more professional jobs. In fact, this is already happening in medicine (e.g., Medicast), programming (e.g., Elance), and law (e.g., Axiom), among others. The on-demand economy is already affecting incumbent industries and altering the labor market in cities around the globe. Yet this form of indie urbanpreneurship is only in its infancy, and the potential long-term impacts and opportunities are only just beginning to emerge.

## INDIE URBANPRENEURS: MAKERS

Some indie urbanpreneurs are inventors, or makers, tapping into other collaborative resources of the city such as 3D printing labs or Fab Labs where they can utilize things like laser cutters and high-tech prototyping tools without paying to own them outright. They participate in meetups in their communities to network with, and learn from, other indie urbanpreneurs, creators, artists, and developers to get ideas and share experiences. In the past few years several books have been written about the maker movement including *The Maker Movement Manifesto* by Mark Hatch and *Makers: The New Industrial Revolution* by Chris Anderson. Previously referred to as the Do-It-Yourself movement, makers like to tinker and innovate new items, usually for themselves, friends, or families. Yet, the introduction of two-sided platforms connecting producers and potential consumers has opened up new windows of opportunity for makers to convert their hobbies into careers as what I refer to as indie maker urbanpreneurs.

Shenzhen, China, has been emerging as a formidable player in the entrepreneurial ecosystem for the development of hardware products. As a result, Shenzhen has a burgeoning maker movement represented by member groups such as Shenzhen Do-It-Yourself (SZDIY). Increasingly younger educated, urban professionals in Shenzhen are shunning work in multinationals for the excitement and fun of joining the maker movement:

Soon after computer engineer Terry Ouyang finished university, he found there was plenty of work with industry behemoths such as IBM. But it wasn't long before he ditched the corporate ladder to make hardware on his own terms.

"Our generation's motivation is different," Ouyang told CNN. "Our parents were focused on making a living. But we want to do interesting and original things. Instead of making things for other companies, we want to make things ourselves."[18]

Perhaps the most well-known maker, especially in the United States, is Limor Fried, who in 2012 was awarded "Entrepreneur of the Year" by *Entrepreneur Magazine*. Fried started her maker efforts in her apartment, but later expanded her maker business, Adafruit, to a Manhattan warehouse. Adafruit designs and develops hundreds of electronic projects, frequently customized for the consumer, in their 15,000 square foot project. Ms. Fried's company, which was ranked as the fastest growing manufacturing company in New York City by *Inc Magazine* in 2014, embraces open-source hardware that they define as

design is made publicly available so that anyone can study, modify, distribute, make and sell the design or hardware based on that design. The hardware's source, the design from which it is made, is available in the preferred format for making modifications to it. Ideally, open source hardware uses readily available components and materials, standard processes, open infrastructure, unrestricted content, and open-source design tools to maximize the ability of individuals to make and use hardware. Open source hardware gives people the freedom to control their technology while sharing knowledge and encouraging commerce through the open exchange of designs. If any of our products include software or firmware to operate, we also provide all of the source code for your hacking pleasure.[19]

Do-It-Yourselfers have existed throughout history, but with the introduction of new technologies like 3D printers, online platforms for connecting with customers, and crowdfunding platforms, the maker movement is poised to expand dramatically, potentially even outside of this world. NASA experts are anticipating 3D modeling as the key enabler for the emergence of "cities" in Mars.

One of the largest online platforms for the maker movement is Etsy. Etsy was founded by Rob Kalin in an apartment in Brooklyn in 2005 as a platform for connecting artists, artisans, and makers with potential customers around the globe. Etsy has experienced impressive growth. As of April 2015, Etsy had 685 employees, 29 million items for sale from 1.4 million active makers, and nearly 20 million active buyers. According to their website, they also facilitated 1.93 billion (USD) in purchases in 2014, with revenues approximately 10 percent of total sales (195 million USD). Etsy is a certified B Corporation that demonstrates a strong commitment to social and environmental impact of their business while also helping local economies and local makers around the globe. In April 2015, Etsy issued an initial public offering (IPO) where they raised about 267 million (USD).[20] Not everything about Etsy is rosy, however. First of all, the stock price since the IPO dropped significantly from $16 a share to under $14.18 in October 2015, making it the worst performing IPO of the year.[21] That is not all the bad news for Etsy either. As it has scaled, Etsy has managed to alienate many of the crafters/makers who made Etsy what it is. The feel-good, handmade authenticity has given way to problems of credibility and scale, with businesses like Three Bird Nest being accused of using Etsy as a platform for selling "hand-made-in-China" clothing. With cases like Three Bird Nest and Etsy's recent IPO, Etsy and other similar platforms are struggling to balance growth with maintaining the indie credibility, which is a source of success in the first place. The challenges for sharing platforms as they scale to ensure they stay true to what got them traction will be discussed in depth in our final chapter.

While makers could technically live anywhere in the world given the online platforms connecting them to funding and customers, I believe we will see the biggest growth in maker entrepreneurs in urban settings. One main reason for this is that makers who increasingly rely on advanced 3D printing technology will have more shared access to this and other related technologies in urban spaces such as Hacker Lab in Sacramento referenced earlier in this chapter. Actually some cities are collaborating with the maker community to drive the growth of the maker movement. For example, San Diego has a Makers Quarter, which forms part of East Village, home to several makerspaces including the Coliseum, Silo, Smarts Farm, and a Fab Lab.

Fab Labs represent a growing movement, started by MIT, for more advanced shared makerspaces. For a makerspace to be considered for membership into the Fab Lab Network it must meet several requirements regarding openness and accessibility to the local community, technology tools available (including 3D printers, laser cutters, milling machines, and much more), and a commitment to sharing learning locally and with the Fab Lab Network around the globe:

The Fab Lab Network is an open, creative community of fabricators, artists, scientists, engineers, educators, students, amateurs, professionals, ages 5 to 75+, located in more than 40 countries in approximately 200 Fab Labs. From community based labs to advanced research centers, Fab Labs share the goal of democratizing access to the tools for technical invention. This community is simultaneously a manufacturing network, a distributed technical education campus, and a distributed research laboratory working to digitize fabrication, inventing the next generation of manufacturing and personal fabrication.[22]

Aside from markets like Etsy for makers of all types to promote their products to consumers around the globe, and Fab Labs and other makerspaces that encourage tinkering and sometimes entrepreneurs emerge, new entities are emerging that merge both the coworking fabrication facilities with online platforms for makers to connect with potential customers. Imprima3D based in São Paulo, Brazil, is one such example. Imprima3D seeks to be an incubator for makers by assisting with education on how to use their 3D printers, assisting with determining what kind of products customers might want, and then utilizing their platform to connect 3D makers with customers throughout Brazil. Shapeways also offers both a printing service and an online marketplace to a global audience. In 2015, Shapeways claimed more than 10,000 makers who utilize their printers and marketplace around the globe.

## DIGITAL INDIES

I started this chapter highlighting the general trends, especially among millennials, toward freelancing as this generation and others are drawn to the freedom of this form of independent entrepreneurial activity. Freelancing has existed for decades and will only continue to grow in the future. While there are many forms of truly independent freelancing where technically the need to be near other people is minimal at best, I believe going forward most independent freelancers will choose cities over rural environments, following similar trends among the broader population. Increasingly, people are looking for access to the arts and culture, quality infrastructure, opportunities to meet like-minded professionals, leisure activities, and the many other factors drawing people to cities around the world. In a 2015 article, Emma Siemasko framed it this way while also asking the following question:

The self-employed can work wherever they desire. They can travel the world and freelance from a beachside tiki bar, or stay in their hometown close to family and friends. Since having a reliable Internet connection is your only requirement, what are the best cities to live in if you're a full-time freelancer?[23]

In case you are wondering, her top five choices, all in the United States were Portland, Oregon; Austin, Texas; Nashville, Tennessee; Miami, Florida and Los Angeles, California. Her rationale was varied and not based on an in-depth set of criteria, but included references to high numbers of freelancers, cost of living and tax rates, size of arts scene, and weather.

## THE SHIFT TOWARD CHEAP OR FREE ICT

As discussed in the opening chapter, the democratization of innovation and technology is having a big impact on entrepreneurial ecosystems around the globe. Software has been trending to zero with open-source tools, Word Press, and many others while cloud computing is eliminating the need for dedicated servers for many digital entrepreneurs. Today, cities are adding new ICT resources to the mix, which serve as platforms for innovation opportunities. Open data and sensor networks, for example, can serve as the raw material for app developers and digital entrepreneurs to develop solutions for local or global markets.

The story of Markus Frind and his wildly successful dating site experiment provides a great example of this type of Digital Indie Urbanpreneur type. Frind grew up on a farm in a small town in British

Columbia, 14 hours from Vancouver. He later moved to Vancouver, where he got a technical degree in computer programming. While in Vancouver, he began working for several Internet start-ups, most of whom were crashing during the difficult days in the industry post the dot-com bust. In a desire to test some programming skills and possibly breaking free of being an employee in yet another dot com, Frind decided to start a no-frills dating site, he called Plenty of Fish in 2004. While there were several entrenched players in the industry at that time, Frind was an early mover in trying to create a free site. Monetization would hopefully come later once a critical mass of users were coming to the site. *Inc Magazine* did a cover story about Frind and Plenty of Fish in 2009:

Five years ago, he started Plenty of Fish with no money, no plan, and scant knowledge of how to build a Web business. Today, according to the research firm Hitwise, his creation is the largest dating website in the U.S. and quite possibly the world. Its traffic is four times that of the dating pioneer Match, which has annual revenue of $350 million and a staff that numbers in the hundreds. Until 2007, Frind had a staff of exactly zero. Today, he employs just three customer service workers, who check for spam and delete nude images from the Plenty of Fish website while Frind handles everything else.[24]

Plenty of Fish grew its user base rapidly and Frind was able to take advantage of Google's Adsense program to monetize the growing volume of aspiring daters. After meeting a tech blogger at a local conference, and sharing with him that Frind was making 10,000 (USD) a day from ads on his site, the blogger didn't buy it. And a mini-scandal started brewing in Vancouver as a result. Frind, in an attempt to prove his claim, posted a picture of himself with a check from Google for about 800,000 (Canadian dollars) for two months of ad revenue from the Adsense program. This scandal only served to draw more users to the site. By 2009, Plenty of Fish was raking in $10 million a year in revenue with virtually no employees and his own computer in his Vancouver apartment functioning as the company server.

Why is Frind's story interesting, to me at least? Of course, there is the obvious wonder at how a guy with no founding team, no start-up capital, and no plan (not even a business model canvas) was able to build up a company generating that kind of revenue from his home. But there were a few instances in the story I shared, where you can see that Frind's location in Vancouver (and not, for example, his original hometown of Hudson's Hope) contributed to the success of his independent enterprise.

First, he was able to work directly in the local Internet start-up space. In fact, he worked for six different dot-com start-ups in Vancouver in a span of a few years. So the density of Internet start-ups in Vancouver contributed to Frind learning new tech skills and of course building his network. Also the fact that Vancouver hosted a tech conference that he could attend, and then meet a blogger who inadvertently assisted Frind in building a bigger user base, also contributed to his success. Another more subtle aspect of at least this type of independent entrepreneur, that is, of relevance, is the access to high bandwidth Internet as his site grew. This example of digital infrastructure in cities is becoming increasingly important.

In early 2015, I was asked to deliver a keynote at the Gigabit Cities Summit in Kansas City. Kansas City was the first city in North America to receive a commitment to implement Google Fiber, and this summit was focused on bringing together thought leaders and other communities around North America who are trying to determine how to leverage high-speed broadband to attract and retain innovators and entrepreneurs to their communities. Plenty of Fish is a great example of the type of independent enterprise that could be attracted to a community where high bandwidth exists. As the site grew in user base, it also grew in the volume of data it was streaming around the globe as the hundreds of thousands of users posted pictures or even videos in hopes of finding a mate.

## SHOULD CITIES SEEK TO ATTRACT INDIE URBANPRENEURS TO THEIR CITIES?

Throughout this chapter I have shared insights regarding the drivers for the emergence of this space as well as highlighted several types of indie urbanpreneurs such as makers, on-demand urbanpreneurs, and freelance/ digital urbanpreneurs. I happen to believe that this is a positive trend for cities and for the entrepreneurial movement globally. Yet, some of my economist friends think otherwise. Economists are used to measuring the impact of innovation and entrepreneurship in terms of job growth and local economic development. While stories like that of Frind and Plenty of Fish or Gepper's Coolest Cooler abound, these projects in and of themselves have little impact on a region's economic development and even less on job growth. Between just those two examples I suspect that even today they don't account for more than 20–30 jobs. Yet the two of them have created innovations that have generated well over 10 million (USD) each (in the case of Frind, recent reports I have heard suggest Plenty of Fish is generating over $25 million per year).

Yet I believe urbanpreneurs are a valuable commodity for most any city. First, successful stories like those of Frind and Gepper generate a lot of media attention, and not just for the founder but for the city where they are based. Increasingly, urbanpreneurs are leveraging the invisible infrastructure in cities and the coworking spaces, Fab Labs, and others share in the success of these urbanpreneurs. Cities today compete to create a brand for being an innovation and entrepreneurial hub and these success stories help grow the brand.[25] The London case is highly illustrative. A recent report[26] identified 132 relevant IACs (incubators, accelerators, and coworking spaces) in the city, which at any given time provide support for around 3,800 businesses. This scene is dominated by digital technology ventures (30 percent), communications and publishing (24 percent), designer-makers and product design (15 percent), and production, TV, music, and photography (11 percent). Probably not surprising at this stage, social enterprises are ranked fifth with approximately 380 new purpose-driven ventures using IACs facilities and resources, in London alone.

As the world increasingly becomes a network of cities as opposed to national borders that detract migration, innovators are quite willing to relocate to hotbeds of innovation and entrepreneurship. While in some cases urbanpreneurs, such as Frind, are not likely to create a lot of spinoff opportunities for local suppliers or producers, others just might. Gepper, for example, has expressed little desire to become a manufacturing company. His success with the Coolest Cooler campaign will require licensing the production to manufacturers elsewhere in the region or beyond.

Finally, there are other hidden benefits to the successful indie urbanpreneur movement. Indie urbanpreneurs who are successful could become fantastic mentors or even angel investors in other local urbanpreneurs. As discussed in this chapter and others, the human capital and networking assets in a community are critical to the success of a local entrepreneurial ecosystem. The lessons learned by those who have been successful going it alone could be instrumental in supporting others. And of course there will be some indie urbanpreneurs who won't be able to resist growing their enterprise as demand grows. So some of them will convert from being indie urbanpreneurs to urban tech entrepreneurs, for example. This will lead to more direct benefits in job growth and economic development, which will make the economists happy too.

## CONCLUDING THOUGHTS ON URBANPRENEURS

Recall in the first chapter how I discussed the new role of crowdfunding as a twenty-first-century alternative to equity diluting venture capital.

I also summarized the case of Ryan Gepper, the founder of Coolest Cooler who raised $13 million in a Kickstarter campaign. In a recent *Washington Post* article, Gepper reinforced the point that we are at the convergence of a range of factors from crowdfunding to shared resources such as access to shared maker resources:

We're at a peak time in the creative economy, There are so many things that allow people to translate their ideas into actual, physical products. Things that weren't available even five years ago.[27]

I believe we are at the early stage of a transformation of how work gets done in modern times. We will see more freelancing arrangements replacing formal employment contracts, more makers finding ways to profit from shared resources in cities and leveraging even more ubiquitous technologies to reach local and global audiences all with fewer financial and human resources. These changes will challenge our paradigms of entrepreneurship, venture capital, and corporate jobs. I also believe these trends will challenge traditional economic views of the role of entrepreneurship in an economy and what kinds of public policy should be implemented to encourage it. I hope you are strapped in, because we are in for a wild ride.

# CHAPTER 5

## Big City Enablers

As Margaret Thatcher put it "Economics are the method; the object is to change the heart and soul." But, we can look at a city differently. We could choose to believe that "Head, heart and soul are the method; the object is to change the economy." We can choose to see the city as a collection of people who have converged on a specific location because it offers them opportunities to do the things that they want to do, to be the person that they want to be and fulfill their potential. . . . Where an economy is produced that serves people, both now and into the future.[1]

This chapter is dedicated to discussing emerging practices that seek to encourage different forms of urban entrepreneurship in cities around the globe.. This will include a focus on how cities support the development of the next generation of urban entrepreneurs through public school education, treating the city as an urban laboratory to test new innovations and demand-side policies, leveraging concepts from open innovation and the sharing economy such as civic crowdsourcing in procurement. I will also explore the emergence of chief innovation officers in leading cites around the globe and discuss how some of these cities are purposefully creating and supporting the invisible infrastructure of coworking spaces, incubators and accelerators, and 3D labs. Finally, I will explore how cities such as Amsterdam and Seoul, South Korea, are proactively supporting the creation of sharing economy start-ups and infrastructure to support urbanpreneurship and reduce their environmental footprints while addressing inequality by facilitating access to products and services not normally accessible to all economic classes.

In *Welcome to the Urban Revolution* (2009), my friend Jeb Brugmann demonstrated that innovation and entrepreneurship is becoming a largely urban phenomenon and that countries wanting to succeed in growing their innovation and entrepreneurial economy need to focus more effort on boosting urban innovation and entrepreneurial ecosystems. Brugmann presented a convincing case that cities, not nation-states, are the key to innovation in the global economy and that innovation is diffusing more rapidly between cities around the globe, regardless of which country they reside in, of course, once basic levels of sociopolitical and economic stability are achieved.

Much of this book has been dedicated to developing the Urbanpreneur Spiral and documenting the emerging trends associated with different forms of urbanpreneurship spaces and types. It is time to turn my attention to the role of city administration in supporting urbanpreneurship in all its forms. Before introducing examples of emergent practices for fostering each of the two types of urbanpreneurship spaces discussed in this book (civic and indie), I would like to take you through some insights from a study by CITIE (City Initiatives for Technology, Innovation, and Entrepreneurship), which I found fascinating. CITIE is a consortium of global organizations including Nesta from the UK, Accenture consulting, and Catapult Future Cities. Much of the following is derived from their 2015 report but is also complemented from personal conversations I had with the two lead authors, John Gibson, director of Government Innovation for Nesta, and Matthew Robinson, managing director of Policy Research at the Accenture Institute for High Performance.

The CITIE consortium set out to understand how 40 global cities encourage innovation and entrepreneurship. Based on CITIE's extensive global research, they were able to identify nine key policy areas that leading cities adopt to encourage entrepreneurship and innovation. The authors were keen to clarify that although each of the nine policy tools can have positive impacts on the local entrepreneurial ecosystem, the tools themselves are not equally valued by the entrepreneurial community. Regardless, the emerging CITIE Framework offers a unique lens for considering the broad policy tools available to cities seeking to increase entrepreneurial activity and to improve their positioning as hotbeds for creative, innovative, entrepreneurial citizens.

As can be observed from their framework (Figure 5.1), the CITIE consortium grouped the nine policy tools into three different components: openness, infrastructure, and leadership.

It would be difficult to disagree with any of their observations based on my ongoing research into what smart and innovative cities are doing to

Figure 5.1   CITIE Framework

promote local entrepreneurship in their community. Aside from the nine policy tools that the CITIE report highlighted, below I will introduce a few other policy tools and activities I have observed cities leveraging to support entrepreneurship, including better tax policy, the introduction of chief innovation officers, and participation in city innovation networks.

## THE BORING TAXES

Ever since scholars and policy makers turned their attention to entrepreneurship as a source of local economic development, one of the first places they have looked to encourage more innovators is through special tax treatment. However, the idea of special taxes to encourage entrepreneurs to locate within particular areas of urban environments is newer.

Barcelona did this with their innovation district, 22@. Buenos Aires followed with their Distrito Tecnologico and offered municipal tax breaks to start-ups locating in the district. San Francisco has also used tax breaks to attract tech companies as part of urban regeneration strategies. The Tenderloin neighborhood, a historically challenged part of San Francisco, was used as a test bed for this strategy. It has worked, arguably too well. Many start-ups, and more established tech heavyweights like Zendesk and Twitter, now call Tenderloin home. I say arguably too successful because there is plenty of local resistance to the increasing domination of the neighborhood by big tech companies.

It is important to note that not all tax policy, even ones intended to help urban entrepreneurs, actually work. The European Union recently introduced a value-added tax (VAT) aimed at curbing the explosive growth of Internet giant retailers from the United States such as Amazon.com while giving local entrepreneurs better opportunities to compete in their home markets. However, the way the law was enacted, home-based makers, artisans, and the like are now also subject to the VAT because the law treats their products sold via online platforms as downloads.[2] I presume this will be rectified since these urbanpreneurs were not the aim of the VAT, but this does illustrate the increasing complexity of tax policy for regions and cities seeking to encourage urbanpreneurship in their communities.

## GOVERNANCE: CHIEF INNOVATION OFFICERS

Cities aspiring to foster vibrant urban entrepreneurial ecosystems need a champion with resources, vision, and capability of supporting the ever-changing needs of the innovation and entrepreneurship community. Just as tech companies have had chief innovation officers in charge of ensuring processes and enabling tools were in place to foster corporate innovation, cities are now hiring their own chief innovation officers. There are literally dozens of such officers just in cities across the United States. Similar roles exist in cities around the globe and I have had the pleasure to interact with many from small towns such as Tigre, Argentina, to megacity officers such as Barcelona, Amsterdam, and Santiago.

In reflecting on whether chief innovation officers will transform government, David Raths, from govtech.com, says:

From Riverside, Calif., to Kansas City, Mo., and from Louisville, Ky., to Massachusetts, states and municipalities are hiring chief innovation officers . . . One trend cities and states are targeting is better ways to use technology.

You see cities creating these *free safety positions*, White said, using a football metaphor. "They can work on alternative ways to do procurement or broker deals across agencies or push for greater use of social media."[3]

Bloomberg Philanthropies has been a big promoter of such cross-cutting initiatives, championing innovation inside and outside city walls. In 2015, Bloomberg announced funding for the creation of i-teams in 12 U.S. cities. For cities to win the funding they had to submit proposals on what innovative challenges they would take on if they won and of course commit to hiring an innovation officer and support staff to execute their projects.

## GOVERNMENT-TO-GOVERNMENT INNOVATION

In 1956, U.S. President Eisenhower introduced Sister Cities International as a tool for fostering urban diplomacy through cultural, educational, and information exchanges between paired cities in the United States and around the globe. Since then, however, cities have increasingly begun to participate in regional or global city networks designed to encourage more rapid diffusion of innovation among cities with similar challenges and aspirations.

Not only are cities aspiring to foster innovation within their own territory but increasingly they are also collaborating with other cities to help them implement similar innovations. Actually one of the criteria for cities to win funding from Bloomberg Philanthropies to fund i-teams was that the project, if successful, could be replicated in other cities and that the i-teams would work to support knowledge transfer and the diffusion of innovation. Cities around the globe have long belonged to networks of cities in the hopes of learning from each other. Some are local or regional while other networks are global. For example, Jeb Brugmann co-founded ICLEI (Local Governments for Sustainability) in 1990 as a city network for sharing emerging practices regarding local sustainable development. Today ICLEI has a membership of more than 1,000 cities in 84 countries. The U.S. Council of Mayors is a nonpartisan membership group for cities with populations over 30,000 with several objectives including facilitating knowledge sharing and promoting best practices among member cities. Europe has the Covenant of Mayors with more than 6,000 mayors who have signed on to a commitment to innovate toward a low-carbon economy and to exceed the EU goal of a 20 percent reduction in $CO_2$ emissions by 2020.[4] RECI (Red Española de Ciudades Inteligentes) is a network of smart cities with over 50 members just in Spain.

In a more recent development some cities are forming consultancies to advise other cities for a fee. As cities embrace innovation and hire chief innovation officers, they are more able to monetize their innovations by helping other cities adapt emerging practices. Edmonton, Canada, has built a reputation for being a North American leader in waste management practices. Recently, Edmonton created Waste Re-Solutions as a for-profit spinoff of the city whose objective is to profit by sharing the city's expertise in waste management to other cities. Waste Re-Solutions was formed with a $1.9 million seed investment and the city's prior waste management manager was hired to run the consultancy.[5] Something similar happened to Barcelona 22@'s team, as Jordi Cabrafiga, former Strategic Sectors and Innovation executive at the Barcelona City Council, referenced in an interview. Back in 2009, Barcelona was already wondering about how to transform all the knowledge developed in setting up the project into profitable spinoffs. And it seems that the idea worked. In a 10-year retrospective report, they emphasize:

22@Barcelona today is a benchmark of urban, economic and social transformation for cities like Rio de Janeiro, Boston, Istanbul and Cape Town. This model is studied and followed by Science and Technology Parks around the world. The experience of the Innovation District has been used as a model in other districts of the city, which are taking advantage of the accumulated know-how. On a territorial level, the 22@ Economic Promotion team is already working to drive the economy of la Sagrera and to transform the economy of Zona Franca, among others.[6]

## EMERGING PRACTICES FOR STIMULATING TECH, INDIE, AND CIVIC URBANPRENEURSHIP

The focus of this chapter so far has been on broad models and approaches to stimulating innovation and entrepreneurship in cities. The rest of this chapter is focused on emerging practices for stimulating the great migration and the two forms of urbanpreneurship spaces discussed in this book: indie urbanpreneurship and civic entrepreneurship.

## STIMULATING THE GREAT MIGRATION

### From STEM to STEAM Education

Much of the innovation and entrepreneurship discussed in this book is directly associated with ICT and other technology development.

Even many of the urban entrepreneurial projects discussed, such as artisans selling customized products via Etsy, are leveraging emerging technology platforms to reach their markets. Clearly as we move forward, technology acumen is going to be a key skillset for most entrepreneurs and for society as a whole. The challenge for cities, then, is how to ensure that citizens of all income classes are capable of participating in modern innovation economies.

One of the most important approaches to address this challenge is through STEM education. STEM stands for science, technology, engineering, and mathematics education. The idea of STEM education is to ensure that youth gain early and regular access to the tools that will shape innovation and entrepreneurship in the twenty-first century so that they will be better prepared and inspired to seek advanced education and careers in these fields. Not all STEM education is dependent on school boards and city administrators. There are civic entrepreneurs who have been keen to support the adoption of STEM education. For example, in 1998, Dean Kamen founded First Lego League (FLL) as a "powerful program that engages children in playful and meaningful learning while helping them discover the fun in science and technology."[7] FLL involves parents and children, ages 9 to 14, in the process of applying science and technology to overcome a range of simple and complex challenges.

Outgoing U.S. President Obama is well aware of the growing innovation gaps in the United States compared with other countries around the world and has been a big advocate in promoting the adoption of STEM education. He has also invested significantly, committing more than 3 billion (USD) to address the skills gap by embracing corporate leaders in getting insights on the needed STEM skills, funded a program to educate 100,000 STEM teachers, and focused attention on underserved youth like minorities and girls.

Let's also make sure that a high school diploma puts our kids on a path to a good job. Right now, countries like Germany focus on graduating their high school students with the equivalent of a technical degree from one of our community colleges, so that they're ready for a job. At schools like P-Tech in Brooklyn, a collaboration between New York Public Schools, the City University of New York, and IBM, students will graduate with a high school diploma and an associate degree in computers or engineering.[8]

The Brookings Institution's report on innovation districts introduced earlier in the book also placed significant emphasis on the role of STEM education in helping to transform cities into engines of innovation.

Cities and metropolitan areas are experimenting with new approaches to economic development and sustainable development that focus on growing jobs in productive, innovative, and traded sectors of the economy while concurrently equipping residents with the skills-particularly STEM skills-they need to compete for and succeed in these jobs.[9]

Brookings went on to document the focus most innovation districts place on STEM education in the local community. Because many innovation districts emerge in neglected parts of cities, local residents are frequently lower income. Cities that proactively seek to avoid displacement of these residents while transforming poor neighborhoods into innovation districts can place a priority on STEM education for the lower income population.

## FROM STEM TO (E)STEAM

More recently there is a movement to expand the STEM concept and to convert it to STEAM adding in the arts to the curriculum. The Rhode Island School of Design (RISD) was among the first to introduce the STEAM concept and have argued that arts and design are critical tools for innovators in modern times. This is an important contribution to the STEM discussion, clearly aligned with Richard Florida's work on the creative class, and a movement that should be followed closely by cities seeking to embrace modern, interdisciplinary innovation and entrepreneurship in a holistic way. At the time of this writing, the organization STEM to STEAM had identified more than 1,200 research, education, policy, and industry groups in the United States who have embraced the broader STEAM curriculum as a way to close the gap in core youth education to prepare them for the challenges and opportunities in the decades to come.

Early in 2015, I was invited to give a keynote at a smart cities event in Brussels. During that keynote I spoke about my observation that we three generations of the smart cities movement have emerged. Smart Cities 1.0 involved multinational technology companies trying to sell their existing products and services to the municipal market. Smart cities 2.0 involved cities recognizing that this smart cities thing could be an important tool for transforming cities but that the city administrators, not the tech companies, need to take leadership to assess needs and then solicit innovations from the private sector. Smart Cities 3.0 involves citizen co-creation whereby cities serve as a platform for the civic hackers and urban entrepreneurs to take more ownership over the future of their cities.

In this 3.0 version I referenced the importance of STEM and STEAM education in creating smarter citizens more capable of participating in the 3.0 version.

Unbeknownst to me, I was to later be on a panel with Crystal Glangchal, founder of Venture Lab based in San Antonio, Texas. When Crystal's turn on the panel came up, I was surprised to hear that not only is she a guru in STEAM education and founded Venture Lab to bring STEAM to youth, especially girls, but she has also pioneered the concept of E(STEAM). The E stands for entrepreneurship and what Venture Lab aims to do is teach "young people to be next generation innovators and entrepreneurs through inspiration, experiential learning and mentorship" (venturelab.org). This was the first and only time I have heard of E(STEAM) education, but you can imagine, I am a fan. Helping educate our youth to not only have the core knowledge required to be innovators but also helping them learn the tools to turn their innovative ideas into viable projects and become future urbanpreneurs is a fantastic idea.

Venture Lab is part of a growing movement of civic innovators who are forming tech education facilities to help bridge the digital divide and assist cities in growing the digital workforce from within, including digital entrepreneurs. The Centre for London refers to these start-ups as Digital Learning Programmes and has identified 60 such digital education start-ups in East London alone![10] Thus, civic entrepreneurs are yet again demonstrating their capacity to recognize urban challenges and find entrepreneurial solutions to close the gap, alleviating pressure on city administrators to solve every problem on their own. Smart cities would find incentives to encourage the growth of these digital divide bashers as a complement to efforts to improve the public education efforts for STEM, STEAM, and E(STEAM).

## INNOVATION DISTRICTS

In 2012, I took a job as the director of the Center for Entrepreneurship at a private university in Buenos Aires. One of my first responsibilities was to build a vision for how the university could support our current and former entrepreneurial alumni and plug our university into the regional entrepreneurial ecosystem. I was given some latitude and a little budget to go on a mission to explore how other universities do this in other parts of the world. Not surprisingly, I chose Boston as my key destination. I was able to meet with people at MIT and Harvard as well as with incubators and accelerators such as the Cambridge Innovation Center, Tech Stars Boston, and Mass Challenge. Mass Challenge has been located in Boston's Innovation District from its start in 2009 and has incubated 617 start-ups in its first 5 years. The rapid uptake in office space in the Innovation District has led to rising rents and more demand for tech start-up space throughout the city. New districts are starting to pop up throughout the city and Boston has even initiated a new program called the Neighborhood Innovation District to further support the distributed nature of the tech start-up scene throughout the city.

In Chapter 2, I introduced the emergence of innovation districts as an alternative to suburban tech parks like Silicon Valley and Route 128 in Boston. Innovation districts are frequently developed in rundown parts of a city in hopes of spurring urban regeneration while simultaneously growing the entrepreneurial ecosystem. On page 1 of the Brookings report, they highlight the uniqueness of innovation districts as an economic development tool for cities:

Innovation districts represent a radical departure from traditional economic development. Unlike customary urban revitalization efforts that have emphasized the commercial aspects of development (e.g., housing, retail, sports stadiums), innovation districts help their city and metropolis move up the value chain of global competitiveness by growing the firms, networks, and traded sectors that drive broad-based prosperity. Instead of building isolated science parks, innovation districts focus extensively on creating a dynamic physical realm that strengthens proximity and knowledge spillovers. Rather than focus on discrete industries, innovation districts represent an intentional effort to create new products, technologies and market solutions through the convergence of disparate sectors and specializations (e.g., information technology and bioscience, energy, or education).[11]

Perhaps the most recognized innovation district to date is that of 22@ in Barcelona. Barcelona was one of the first cities in the world to embrace the concept of an innovation district. 22@, a former industrial district, had fallen into disrepair as industrial operations were phased out of the city toward the middle and end of the twentieth century. Seeking an infusion of private investment and a growth in the tech start-up community in the city, Barcelona's City Council hatched the idea of turning this derelict district into a high-tech hub of commerce and education. They started by investing heavily in high-speed bandwidth throughout the district and constructing a few iconic buildings in 22@ to house city innovation hubs, incubators, and some staffing. Barcelona bet the farm, investing over 180 million euros since the launch of 22@ in 2000. The original target for 22@ was primarily to leverage the attractiveness of

Barcelona as a place to live, lower cost of living, and significant university infrastructure and student body to attract multinational tech companies like Microsoft, Google, Yahoo, and Intel to set up European offices in the district. The hope was that this would also lead to spillover effects and encourage new tech companies to form and locate in 22@.

While the city has managed to entice several multinational firms to enter, including Microsoft, Cisco, and Siemens in recent years, 22@ has thrived as a hub for emerging tech start-ups. Ten years after its founding, the city reports that 22@ now hosts more than 7,000 companies and 56,000 employees. While some companies previously existed in Barcelona or other parts of Europe, and have been enticed to move to the district to the lower rent, access to the digital infrastructure, or collaboration opportunities with other like-minded companies, the city reports that about 500 new companies are founded in 22@ each year. 22@ was the inspiration for the design and implementation of innovation districts in Buenos Aires, Boston, and Medellín.

Boston's latest initiative, the Neighborhood Innovation District, may actually represent the next big trend in innovation clusters in cities. As opposed to trying to house all, or most, of an entrepreneurial and innovation ecosystem in a larger city in just one area, the concept behind the Neighborhood Innovation District is to distribute a city's innovation potential throughout the city by facilitating smaller, neighborhood-scale developments. Boston's latest mayor, Martin Walsh, launched this initiative toward the end of 2014, in part to reduce the space and pricing pressure being felt in their innovation district due to its overwhelming success. This strategy can also allow the city to harness more its innovation potential and to support ongoing regeneration efforts throughout the city, as opposed to focus them in a singular location. The first step taken was the creation of a city-wide, interdisciplinary team, the Neighborhood Innovation District Committee whose goal is to

expand innovation and entrepreneurship in the City of Boston. The Neighborhood Innovation District Committee will seek to identify policies, practices, and infrastructure improvements to support the development of innovation districts throughout the City.[12]

While hosting neighborhood-scale innovation districts throughout a city may not always be necessary for smaller cities, I think it could be quite useful for the megacities around the globe. Given the other trends discussed throughout this book such as the decreasing costs of ICT and related technology, and the use of coworking spaces and shared 3D labs and Fab Labs, it is easy to envision cities such as Barcelona, Boston, Hong Kong, London, New York City, San Francisco, and Tokyo embracing a distributed network of neighborhood innovation districts throughout their cities.

Being located in a country of constant economic crisis has certainly not helped Buenos Aires achieve its potential as a hub of innovation. In fact, after consulting to the city for 1 year on their smart cities strategy, I published an article asking if it was possible to be a smart city in a stupid country. Of course, I made few friends with Argentinian immigration officials with that article, but in my work with the city it was clear that there were significant national and political barriers to achieving its ambitious smart city agenda. Furthermore, the ongoing economic uncertainty in the country has led to both a brain drain and capital flight. Despite all this, Buenos Aires continues to strive to be an attractive place for local entrepreneurs (I think they have largely given up hope of attracting regional or global entrepreneurs in the current environment).

Yet Buenos Aires has already experimented with a similar model to 22@ whereby they have their core technology innovation district (Distrito Tecnologico) but also several other innovation districts focused on other clusters such as an audiovisual cluster (Distrito Audiovisual), design district (Distrito de Diseño), and an arts district (Distrito de las Artes). Outside of the Distrito Tecnologico, the other districts were formed roughly near existing clusters of business in those fields. I am not convinced that a cluster model will always make sense for cities as they may not want to try to force cluster development and instead support each neighborhood to evolve their district as they see fit. This leads into the next topic of how cities are increasingly leveraging concepts of open innovation as a way to solve city challenges and embrace citizens and start-ups to be part of the solution.

## STIMULATING CIVIC ENTREPRENEURSHIP AND CIVIC TECH

Nesta, a lead contributor to the CITIE report discussed above, and the United Kingdom's leading innovation agency, suggested that 2014 was the year of social innovation in cities, suggesting that by the end of the year, all UK cities would likely have a strategy for social innovation. While their bold claim was not completely fulfilled, the recognition by cities that civic innovation is a necessity and that local entrepreneurs will necessarily play an important role in helping to transform cities for the better is spot on.

The National League of Cities recently developed a list of approaches cities can take to encourage civic innovators. Specifically, the National League of Cities identified three approaches: building the right channels to listen to citizens, responding directly to public demand, and getting the community on board.

The rapid growth of social networks has its downsides when considering how cities can engage citizens in the manner recommended by the National League of Cities. Should cities use Twitter, Facebook, websites, or offline tools like town hall meetings to discover concerns and ideas from its citizens? I would say all of the above and more. It is not possible to reach a broad enough spectrum of citizens using one or two communication channels. Some citizens, such as the elderly, may not easily be reached using online tools, requiring face-to-face interactions. Others, of course, exclusively prefer digital communication tools. In fact, in recent years, civic tech innovators have introduced dozens, probably hundreds, of different tools for facilitating dialog between cities and their citizens. Philadelphia uses Philly311; Tallahassee, Florida, uses DigiTally; and cities around the globe use several other tools such as See-Click-Fix for citizen reporting of problems and tools such as Australia's OurSay for mobile engagement between citizens and their representatives.

Seoul, South Korea, uses a platform called 10 million Imaginations, which after the first two years of use had received visits from more than 4 million residents and had registered more than 33,000 ideas.[13] After receiving the ideas through the platform, citizen committees evaluate the ideas and recommend the best ideas for consideration by the city. Eventually the best ideas are presented by the civic innovator and some are implemented and the innovator receives cash compensation.

Another such example worth mentioning is the process embraced by the City of Vancouver, Canada, in its effort to build a vision for the future. In 2009, with the assistance of 60 city staff and Mayor Gregor Robertson's vision, the city embarked on a massive outreach campaign, leveraging online tools and town hall meetings in an attempt to create a shared vision for the future of the city. The range of outreach initiatives led to the contribution of 30,000 citizens in the creation of the Greenest City Action Plan. Through this collaboration Vancouver developed a bold set of strategies to achieve a stretch goal of becoming the greenest city in the world by 2020. Goals were set for the creation of green jobs, increased use of public transit, access to green space, and increased development and use of renewable energy.

## CIVIC INCUBATORS

In the chapter on civic entrepreneurs I wrote about the factors driving entrepreneurs to address problems in their local communities. While my research with Pablo demonstrates that this breed of entrepreneur is quite common and that they are accustomed to seeking collaborations with local governments, there is plenty more local governments can do to directly encourage civic entrepreneurs. Cities around the globe are creating incubators specifically geared toward solving civic challenges. My favorite example of this is Boston's New Urban Mechanics. I will reflect on some of the insights I got from interview with Nigel Jacob, one of the cofounders of the incubator, in the section devoted to urban labs. Bear with me.

## OPEN CIVIC INNOVATION

Governments used to think of citizens as passive recipients, and hopefully beneficiaries, of local government action (i.e., customers). In recent years, however, forward-thinking governments are embracing the distributed innovation potential of citizens. While there are probably dozens of ways local governments have started to embrace open innovation, let me tackle two specific approaches: (1) open data and hackathons and (2) civic crowdsourcing.

### Open Data and Hackathons

Local governments have access to massive amounts of data about everything ranging from business licenses and crime reports to aggregate health and education information of the population. As technology continues to evolve, cities are gaining even more data, in real time on items such as traffic congestion and air contamination from sensors placed throughout the city. In partnership with IBM, Rio de Janeiro was one of the first cities in the world to embrace all of this real-time data to create a centralized operations center that monitors all of these data in real time and is able to respond to emergencies and, in some cases, prevent emergencies from their operations center. The original concept for the center was to find ways to prevent more deaths in Favelas resulting from landslides. IBM and Rio implemented a system of humidity sensors and warning systems to alert local residents when the danger levels of landslides was high.

The Rio Operations Center has gone well beyond warning residents of weather events. I spoke with a colleague from IBM (Stephen Ouellette) a few years ago about the Operations Center and asked him for a concrete example of how this initiative has contributed to improved quality of life.

Here was his answer:

In January 2012, a 20-story office building next to the municipal theatre in downtown Rio de Janeiro collapsed. The operations center took immediate action: alerting the fire and civil defence departments and working with the local gas and electric companies to shut down service surrounding the building. The center's employees also halted the underground subway, diverted traffic, secured the site and nearby buildings, and alerted local hospitals. The center used its Twitter feed to alert Rio citizens about the incident, helping divert people away from the site and pre-empting traffic congestion.

The use of real-time data in Rio is primarily focused on one-way communication and services from the city to citizens. Yet, many cities around the globe are finding ways to make all these data freely available to citizens and companies to use in ways that can improve the quality of life of local residents. In other words, cities are leveraging open innovation by opening their data so that others can find innovative uses of these data. Helsinki, Finland, for example, has more than 1,000 open data sets for public use relating to city planning, construction, culture, economy, environment, health, housing, and jobs among others.

Buenos Aires has been an early leader in the provision of open data in Latin America. Buenos Aires currently offers more than 120 open data sets. Furthermore, the city regularly hosts hackathons designed to encourage local citizens and developers to actively use the data to create apps that might be of use to the community. The Buenos Aires open data portal shows 23 current mobile apps, mostly developed by citizens, which leverage their open data sets. These apps range from identifying the nearest public Wi-Fi hotspots to finding the nearest cycling paths and car parking spots.

## Civic Crowdsourcing

One of the most exciting ways cities are embracing open innovation is through something I refer to as civic crowdsourcing. The idea is to change how local governments identify and procure new innovations. The traditional way is to be quite bureaucratic with what the local government requires using cumbersome request for proposal (RFP) procedures and detailed specifications. These traditional processes usually result in less innovation and primarily benefit large corporations capable of dealing with the costly and timely process to submit proposals to local governments.

Civic crowdsourcing, or procurement for innovation, is designed to address these major inefficiencies in traditional procurement and encourage more local government innovation. Together with two of my research colleagues in Canada, Jan Kietzmann and John Pripic, we developed a model demonstrating the potential for civic crowdsourcing to transform how local governments procure innovations. Using existing government practices, we demonstrated that there is a range of procurement approaches from tactical to strategic to market escalation and finally to civic idea crowdsourcing. Our model suggests that local governments may choose to use any of these approaches depending on a set of factors including the maturity of the problem, the maturity of known solutions, and the objectives of the specific procurement activity. If the need is basic and the solutions are prevalent, tactical procurement with narrowly defined specifications may be just fine. However, when there are no obvious or clear solutions, and the city seeks to stimulate innovative solutions to problems identified by the citizens or the city staff, utilizing crowdsourcing to generate ideas and fund the development of truly innovative solutions is most appropriate.

## BCN OPEN CHALLENGE

Barcelona, Spain, has been an early pioneer in this practice, most notably with their recent project called BCN Open Challenge. Instead of predetermining the specifications of desired solutions, the Ayuntamiento de Barcelona identified six challenges and posted them in Catalan, Spanish, and English on a global ideas platform for cities (Citymart.com). Barcelona received 119 proposals from citizens and companies around the globe and are in the process of contracting the winners to implement their innovative proposals.

## LONDON CROWDSOURCING

In early 2015, London's Mayor Boris Johnson launched a civic crowdsourcing program to make London a smarter city. A press release from the mayor's office summarized the aspirations of the program:

The Mayor of London's Office is today calling on entrepreneurs and innovative businesses to enter a "smart cities" competition that could see their ideas adopted by major regeneration projects across the capital. The Smart London Districts

Challenge-led Innovation Competition is looking for digital technology solutions to help London's growing population better connect with its surroundings
through navigation and "wayfinding" solutions. The smart cities competition is
a partnership between the Mayor of London's Office and the innovation charity
the Institute for Sustainability and involves some of the capital's highest-profile
redevelopment districts, including Battersea Nine Elms, Croydon, Elephant
and Castle, Imperial West and Queen Elizabeth Olympic Park.[14]

## CIVIC CROWDSOURCING IN CHILE

In one of the first projects of this type in Latin America, the Gobierno
Regional de BioBio, together with the World Bank and the Ministry of
Transportation and Telecommunications, developed a civic crowdsourcing program to try to identify new innovations in transportation in the
region. It is called Muevett and it resulted in seven finalists who proposed
a range of innovative ideas to address everything from improving access
to rural patients in emergency situations (911-R) to improving the safety
and security of cyclists (i-BiciPark).

In 2015, Claudio Orrego, the governor for the Santiago region,
announced a funding program as part of the Fondo de Innovacion para la
Competitividad-FIC ("Innovation Fund to Stimulate Competitiveness").
Two funding programs are particularly interesting in their relevance to the
topic of civic crowdsourcing and government open innovation. One is
called Grandes Ideas para una Ciudad Inteligente ("Great Ideas for a
Smarter City") and the other is called Innovacion Social Abierta ("Open
Social Innovation"). In both of these programs, Santiago is looking for universities and other organizations to manage a civic crowdsourcing program
to help the city become smarter. In the Grandes Ideas para una Ciudad
Inteligente, Santiago sought a partner to identify five challenges and then
to foster a call for ideas from 50 or more local SMEs working in digital technology. The best five proposed solutions will then be incubated over about a
12-month period and then delivered for use by the Intendencia and citizens.
In the Innovacion Social Abierta, the program is almost the same, except
that the winning institution will seek to generate proposals from citizens
instead of PYMES. I led a team at my prior university, Universidad del
Desarrollo, in trying to win the right to direct this project and we were
happy to learn our proposal had been selected. As I write this we are building the team to begin the launch of the project.

Crowdsourcing is an open innovation tool in wide use by corporations
and entrepreneurs around the globe, but perhaps its biggest impact may
actually come from local governments who embrace this twenty-first-
century approach to distributed innovation. Civic crowdsourcing, like

the programs being piloted in Chile, pose the potential to improve the quality of life of citizens, and the innovation and efficiency of local government, while also encouraging more active participation from citizens and local companies in their local government.

## CITIES AS A LIVING URBAN LABORATORY FOR URBANPRENEURS

The literature and practice associated with collaborations between the private sector and the public sector is at least decades old. The classical 3P (public-private partnership) explores how companies can support government and ideally civic objectives through different forms of collaboration. The most common form is a traditional outsourcing agreement whereby a government agency outsources a service from the private sector. Classic examples include trash collection, energy generation and distribution, and privatized bus services.

At the Smart City Expo in Barcelona in 2014 I spoke in a panel where one of my copanelists was a senior city administrator. He referred to the classic 3P model from the private sector perspective, "You pay, we profit." Now that was of course tongue-in-cheek, but his point, which has been reinforced by many other city officials I have spoken with, is that the traditional 3P model has too often been driven by profit motives of the private sector partner instead of looking for shared value creation. There are of course good examples of alternative partnership models in the 3P framework. For example, many cities have collaborated with energy efficiency specialists, like Johnson Controls to identify energy savings in municipal buildings. Rather than charge cities significant fees for conducting energy audits and implementing efficiency technologies, efficiency service providers have worked in partnership through what is referred to as an ESCO model (energy service company). With this approach, the ESCO absorbs the costs of the studies and the retrofits and in return obtains a percentage of the energy savings over a period of time long enough to recoup their investment and obtain reasonable profits.

However, in the context of urban and civic entrepreneurship, I have been observing new forms of collaboration that are more complex and involve more actors. In fact, the research Pablo and I did on civic entrepreneurs suggested that this type of actor is often working to create 4P (public-private-people partnerships) as in collaborating with civil society to help achieve common objectives.

There is yet another form, even more complex, and interesting emerging. This is often referred to as the quadruple helix whereby government entities collaborate with the private sector, universities, and civil society to achieve common outcomes.

Many cities have been embracing citizens and entrepreneurs in crowd-sourcing new ideas and solutions to city challenges. The idea of cities serving as living labs to foster innovation and test it at the city level has emerged in the past decade. The European Network of Living Labs (ENOLL) has more than 300 members from cities in Europe and around the globe. ENOLL has been a big supporter of the idea of 4P as a model of direct citizen involvement in local innovation systems, through ideas like participatory budgeting, hackathons, and open app competitions. In some cases, including some of the examples below, cities are enacting what I refer to as the 5P model: public-private-people-professor partnerships. This new "P" explicitly recognizes the importance of engaging local universities in these emergent open innovation ecosystems in smart cities.

## SANTANDER, SPAIN, AS A LIVING LAB

Santander, on the northern coast of Spain, has been making waves in the smart cities movement. Its mayor served as the founding president of the Spanish network of smart cities (RECI) discussed earlier in the chapter. Santander has proposed to join the ENOLL network with an Internet of Things (IoT) living lab. This is consistent with their pioneering work, funded in part by the European Union, to become a "sensing city." Led by city administrators and the Universidad de Cantabria, in 2010 the city embarked on a project to install more than 12,000 sensors throughout the city as an effort to become a smarter city and to serve as a test bed for future smart city applications. The sensors provide real-time measurement of everything from pollution levels and parking availability to trash levels, volume of people on sidewalks, traffic congestion, and humidity levels in public parks. The sensor project has turned Santander into a haven for start-ups and global tech companies seeking to experiment with applications that take advantage of IoT in smart cities. Which is why the collaborators involved aim to solidify their position as a living lab as a member of ENOLL. In their application to ENOLL, the proponents suggest a key goal is to "make our platform a must for the research community, inhabitants and companies wishing to innovate in the smart city framework."[15]

## AMSTERDAM'S 5P STRATEGY: THE AMS INSTITUTE

Amsterdam belongs in this conversation about cities embracing 5P models. In fact, it is a recent development in Amsterdam that started my thinking about 5P models. Amsterdam is already considered one of the smartest cities in the world. I had the pleasure of revisiting Amsterdam last year as a keynote speaker at the annual Smart City Event and was quite impressed with the city's commitment to becoming a smarter, greener city.

One of the most important collaborations in this area is called Amsterdam Smart City, which is "a unique partnership between businesses, authorities, research institutions and the people of Amsterdam." Amsterdam Smart City has supported the creation of dozens of innovation collaborations focused on making the city smarter, but the really inspiring project is one that has only just been launched, the Amsterdam Institute for Advanced Metropolitan Solutions (AMS).

This ambitious project has 50 million euros in support from the City of Amsterdam. It involves a collaboration among two Dutch universities (TU Delft and Wageningen UR), MIT, and independent research group TNO. Also in the collaboration are the City of Boston and several local and international corporations, including Accenture, IBM, Cisco, KPN (the Netherlands' leading telco), Shell, and Waternet (Amsterdam's main water supplier).

This is a 5P project of significant importance. If successful, it will likely be one of the world's best living examples of a 5P model in action. The AMS Institute

aims to become an internationally leading institute where talent is educated and engineers, designers, digital engineers and natural/social scientist jointly develop and valorise interdisciplinary metropolitan solutions. AMS is centred on applied technology in urban themes such as water, energy, waste, food, data and mobility, and the integration of these themes. AMS will develop a deep understanding of the city—sense the city—design solutions for its challenges, and integrate these into the city. In that, Amsterdam is its home base and test bed.[16]

## KANSAS CITY AS A LIVING LAB: INNOVATION PARTNERSHIP PROGRAM

The concept of treating the city as a living lab is not unique to European cities. There are a dozen ENOLL labs in North and South America and a handful in Africa and Asia as well. Furthermore, many cities are embracing the idea of treating the city as a living lab for urban entrepreneurs without joining ENOLL. The New Urban Mechanics office in Boston, which was also replicated in Philadelphia, is one such example. Kansas City has also been making great strides in creating an enabling environment for testing new ideas on the city. The city launched a program called the Innovation Partnership as "a front door for entrepreneurs to apply to develop, test and demonstrate innovative solutions"[17] leveraging city infrastructure as a living laboratory.

RFP365, a local Kansas City start-up, founded by David Hulsen and Stuart Ludlow in 2012, developed a software as a service (SaaS) solution to improve government procurement contracting processes. Through the Innovation Partnership, RFP365 was able to gain access to testing their application on their local government's own procurement processes. Hulsen recognized the value obtained by being allowed to treat Kansas City as an urban lab and to gain early customer feedback:

This is a city that was willing to take a chance on a homegrown solution. The program helped us bypass the bureaucratic hoops, and get in front of the right people at the first meeting. They deserve a lot of credit.[18]

RFP365 now has more than 100 customers in governments around the world.

As you can see, leading cities around the globe are beginning to embrace open innovation by directly supporting the innovative potential of 4P and 5P collaborations involving the public (local government), private (start-ups and multinationals), people (citizen engagement), and professor (local and international university involvement) sectors. While the complexities of such collaboration can be messy, our cities and our citizens should demand nothing less.

## STIMULATING INDIE URBANPRENEURS

For cities seeking to attract and retain indie urbanpreneurs I believe the creation of the invisible infrastructure discussed throughout this book is critical. Recall from Chapter 3 that I have identified three types of indie urbanpreneurs: the maker urbanpreneur, the digital urbanpreneur, and the on-demand urbanpreneur. Cities may adopt strategies to target one, two, or all three types. And some of the aforementioned strategies for attracting other forms of urban entrepreneurs (urban tech and civic) will also contribute to the growth of the indie urbanpreneur by helping to grow the networking assets and soft infrastructure that is of benefit to indie urbanpreneurs as well.

Of particular value to indie urbanpreneurs are things like meetups, the existence of numerous coworking facilities throughout the city, 3D labs and Fab Labs, and the like. Of course, some types of indie urbanpreneurs also need access to good physical infrastructure, particularly high-speed bandwidth.

Returning to Kansas City yet again offers a good example of what cities can do to support indie urbanpreneurs. I have mentioned in other parts of this book that Kansas City was the first city in the United States to obtain the high-speed bandwidth Google Fiber infrastructure. Not content on having just the physical infrastructure, the city realized early on that it needed a plan to capitalize on the physical asset and sought to add the soft or invisible infrastructure layers to allow the city to attract and retain all types of urban entrepreneurs. They developed something called the Playbook, which was a strategy for converting Google Fiber into a competitive advantage for the city, embracing STEM education and technology accelerators and, of course, supporting Google Fiber access to the home to support home-based businesses.

The Economic Development Corporation of Kansas City has been helping the growth of an organic, citizen-led initiative called Kansas City Startup Village.

The first neighborhood to get Google Fiber, known on the map as Hanover Heights but locally as the Kansas City Startup Village, is the new home of early stage startups co-locating near one another to collaborate, leverage resources and to build a community based around growing a tech business.[19]

The Startup Village is receiving further investment from the community and opening up other shared facilities such as Homes for Hackers and a new coworking facility.

Aaron Deacon, managing director of KC Digital Drive, and a personal friend, shared with me some insights on a new initiative, KC Bizcare, and some challenges that have emerged. In private conversations, Deacon shared the following:

KC Bizcare is a city unit (KCMO) designed to help with just such issues. I coordinate a local makerspace roundtable, sort of serving the city in that role, and act as a liaison to the Mayor's Maker Challenge initiative out of the White House. There are certainly good examples here in all three subcategories. A couple of interesting recent examples of tensions—KCMO city hall has been in a showdown with Uber and just voted today on some regulations that Uber says will make them leave; but KCMO says Lyft and a local taxi app service are fine with. Generating quite a lot of local heat.

A couple entrepreneur houses in the Startup Village have gotten special use permits but are having to fight to renew with a hearing Monday, getting some pushback from the neighborhood.[20]

## MAKERSPACES: ADELAIDE, UK

Some cities are taking proactive steps to create collaborative makerspaces and opportunities for digital urbanpreneurs as well. Adelaide in the United Kingdom provides an example. The Adelaide City Council, as part of a modern makeover of its library services, has introduced a Digital Hub, a Media Lab, and an Innovation Lab. The Digital Hub is a space designed to educate the young and the old alike in computer literacy and digital economy opportunities. This of course could help spawn future digital urbanpreneurs in their community. The Media Lab "is a place where digital masterpieces will be created and where the latest equipment and technology will bring to life documentaries, short films, animation, soundscapes, photography and graphic design."[21] Meanwhile the Innovation Lab targets makers by offering shared resources to 3D design and printing, plus workshops and even robotics education. I love this project as it is a way to modernize libraries and complement other STEM or STEAM educational efforts. People don't go to libraries as much as they used to and they don't read books as much as they used to either (I am hoping this book is an exception to that rule). For example, visits to UK libraries dropped nearly 7 percent in a recent 5-year period, meanwhile dozens of libraries in the country have been shut down.[22] But repurposing public resources like libraries, to facilitate access to tools, technologies, and services associated with the knowledge economy is a very smart idea. I hope many other cities embrace this repurposing of the physical space of public libraries and the services that are offered.

Finally, what should cities do about on-demand urbanpreneurs? This is a more complex question. The on-demand economy has been under fire from various stakeholders including local and regional governments and even the on-demand urbanpreneurs. Platforms like TaskRabbit and Uber offer independence and freedom to those who prefer that lifestyle or who find themselves temporarily unemployed. Yet, these platforms have been accused of abusing these on-demand urbanpreneurs and even in many cases skirting the law regarding taxes, benefits, and compensation. My take is that the on-demand economy is absolutely here to stay and, as I mentioned in Chapter 4 on indie urbanpreneurs, is likely to represent an even larger percentage of the total workforce in the future.

Therefore, I recommend cities work with their regional governments and collaborate with other cities to develop regulatory frameworks, which will allow this sector to flourish in a manner that also protects on-demand indie urbanpreneurs' rights.

Cities have largely been caught off-guard by the rapid introduction and penetration of on-demand services in their territories. Not surprisingly, the private sector and civil society have been way ahead of government policy and researchers, resulting in reactionary measures from local governments. For cities interested in supporting the on-demand economy, regulations will need to be put in place that clarify how such service providers and the on-demand indie urbanpreneurs will be taxed, what certifications and insurance will be required, how they will be covered by and support social security systems, and so on.

## REGULATORY TENSIONS

Earlier in this chapter I introduced the insights gleaned from the CITIE research project. The researchers placed importance on how adaptive the city has been to the sharing economy. Economic activity occurring in cities may take many forms and the local government can exert a range of influence from being the primary developer and implementer to serving as an active supporter to being a nonparticipant. Despite the attractiveness and evident relevance of the sharing economy in urban settings, cities are sometimes resistant to certain sharing activities, as has been observed by legal changes brought to Airbnb in New York City and to Uber in Brussels and Kansas City.

The sharing economy is evolving but cities cannot wait for it to mature before acting. In particular, cities need to address the regulatory and taxation issues that the "business end" of the sharing economy has raised. Some cities have banned organisations, such as Uber, for using unregistered drivers. In others there have been fines for breaching local regulations (Barcelona), or new regulations developed to curtail the growth of certain parts of the sharing economy (Berlin). Other cities have worked with sharing economy businesses to find solutions to problems. For example, in Amsterdam, the city council and Airbnb agreed that they would work together to ensure that Airbnb hosts receive guidance on their responsibilities and the rules applicable to them, including a two-month a year limit on renting properties. At the same time, Airbnb will collect and pay the tourist tax to the Council.[23]

While it is easy to be critical of cities that are putting the brakes on some sharing activity, the more I immerse myself in the sharing cities arena, the more I realize it is much more complex than I originally thought. First of all, most sharing economy experts do not even consider Uber to be a sharing economy activity. The main Uber service is really just a private taxi service capable of avoiding labor laws and regulation that traditional taxi services offer. Even Uber executives themselves make an effort to point out that their core service is not part of the sharing economy. To me, the sharing economy is about optimizing underutilized resources and frequently involves peer-to-peer sharing. The further a business model deviates from peer-to-peer sharing of underutilized resources, in general, the further the model is from actually being a contributor to the sharing economy. Airbnb is harder to pin down. Many listings are for renting a room in an inhabited apartment or home. To me that is part of the sharing economy.

But what about investors who acquire apartments in tourist areas of cities and rent the entire units out on an exclusive basis as opposed to actually live in them all or part of the year? When I was updating my indicators for benchmarking smart cities, I planned to add an indicator for how many Airbnb listings were available per capita as a proxy for how supportive a city is of the sharing economy. Then I watched the documentary *Bye Bye Barcelona*, which highlighted the negative impacts Airbnb is having on local residents in tourist neighborhoods like Barceloneta, Las Ramblas, and near Gaudi's Sagrada Familia. Residential buildings were being taken over by these short-term renters, with a disproportionate amount of binge drinkers and night owls. Furthermore, traditional businesses that served locals in those neighborhoods were being pushed out and replaced by souvenir stores, selling products made in China. I have come to realize that there is a real need for cities to encourage more of the ideal sharing of underutilized resources and that smart cities may actually be the ones that do regulate sharing enterprises instead of let them operate free of restrictions.

Portland, Oregon, is one of the first cities in the world to initiate a formal process intended to establish regulations and standards to address the on-demand economy explosion. Their first effort, published on April 9, 2015, focused exclusively on the on-demand transportation providers competing with the incumbent taxi industry such as Uber and Lyft. The city assembled the Portland Private for-hire Transportation Innovation Task Force Report to City Council in order to

review and evaluate the service performance and regulatory framework of Portland's private for-hire transportation (PFHT) industry, and provide guidance and recommendations to the City Council regarding how the industry should evolve and respond to new developments in the industry, including the entry of Transportation Network Companies. The Task Force, assisted by a neutral Facilitator, was asked to study available information, develop written recommendations, and submit its written recommendations to the Commissioner and City Council.[24]

To summarize the Task Force recommendations, on-demand drivers were to be treated with similar regulations as taxi companies with respect to vehicle inspections, background checks, and vehicle permitting with some adaptations to the existing policy regarding insurance requirements, nondiscriminatory practices, fares, fees, vehicle signage, data reporting, and street hailing. The point here is not to dive further into details of specific policy choices but to suggest that cities wishing to embrace the on-demand economy need to get smart about how to regulate the industry in a way that is fair to taxpayers and the on-demand urbanpreneurs. Whether the city should ensure additional protections for incumbent industries (e.g., taxpayers) is another question that of course is debatable.

## SHARING CITIES INITIATIVES

The on-demand economy is regularly considered part of the broader sharing economy. While we are discussing Portland, I reached out to April Rinne, one of the leading consultants and experts on sharing cities policy to get her sense of what the city of Portland is doing to move policy forward in this arena. In private correspondence she stated:

Portland (Oregon) has been an early advocate of the sharing economy in the U.S. In 2013 Portland was one of 15 U.S. cities to sign the Shareable Cities Resolution. In 2014 they were the first city to launch a Shared City partnership with Airbnb, which includes a range of activities from streamlining red tape to emergency trainings and joint tourism campaigns. Mayor Charlie Hales has taken a thoughtful, careful approach to regulatory reform. For example he has clearly stated his support of ridesharing, however unlike many other cities, Portland issued a temporary ban of such services in order to develop an appropriate regulatory strategy to manage them. It is likely that in the long-term this approach will serve the city, its residents and even the platform providers better than an ad hoc, "cobbled together" approach.[25]

In the past few years, the term "sharing cities" has emerged to express the marriage of the sharing economy in urban areas. Two colleagues of mine, Duncan McLaren and Julian Agyeman, recently published the book *Sharing Cities: A Case for Truly Smart and Sustainable Cities.* Furthermore, the Sharing Cities Network, which supports bottom-up, grassroots sharing activity, has grown to include more than 50 cities on six continents. On the policy side, cities like San Francisco, Portland, Amsterdam, and Seoul have taken the lead toward embracing the potential of the sharing economy.

## SHARING CITY SEOUL

Sharing City Seoul, for example, is a vast, ambitious program focused on converting Seoul into the sharing capital of the world. Faced with growing resource constraints and environmental challenges, coupled with a dense population and impressive Internet and smartphone penetration, city leaders recognized a unique opportunity to position the city for a future, sustainable, and connected economy that could further develop a community spirit and improve quality of life for their citizens. The city's strategy has three key components: change laws to support instead of inhibit the sharing economy, provide financial and advisory support to sharing start-ups, and facilitate citizen participation in the sharing economy. Furthermore, the city is taking initiative to lead by example by opening up municipal buildings for public use outside of work hours (nearly 800 buildings so far), providing financial support in several sharing start-ups, opening up more than 1,000 data sets for public use, and creating book- and tool-lending libraries in different neighborhoods throughout the city.

I personally believe the sharing economy in cities is going to have very profound impacts on how we live in cities and also will create significant opportunities for urbanpreneurs, both as new venture opportunities as well as serving as enabling mechanisms for other start-up or indie entrepreneurial activity. Cities that embrace the sharing economy like Seoul and Amsterdam are going to be well positioned to attract and retain the innovators of tomorrow.

Sharing economy models offer major potential to increase access to valuable resources from food and transport to lodging and shared office spaces. There are real opportunities for cities to play a role in facilitating this type of sharing that can create opportunities for community building and local development and even support more social inclusion by helping to provide access to resources that would otherwise be out of the range of lower-income residents. Leftover Swap, for example, allows possessors of excess meals to connect to locals in search of cheap cooked food. The idea for Leftover Swap emerged when its San Francisco–based founder and his friends had ordered too much pizza and did not want to waste it. Several other companies and organizations have emerged in cities around the globe seeking to address the massive food waste in developed countries by redirecting this food to those in need, either for a fee or, in the case of nonprofits, for free. Boulder Food Rescue, for example, recovers leftover foods from bakeries or small grocery stores and delivers the food by bike to local shelters. Cities like Portland, Amsterdam, Barcelona, and Seoul are seeking ways to support this form of sharing while also creating a regulatory environment that seeks to ensure the outcome of more sharing is improved quality of life for more residents.

In early 2016, recognizing all of these trends, and the important transition in leadership happening in Barcelona, I decided to initiate the creation of a sharing economy accelerator for startups interested in collaborating with, as opposed to shirking, local governments. Diego Fernandez, founder of Barcelona's Impact Hub (a network of coworking spaces for entrepreneurs seeking to have positive social and environmental impacts) joined forces with me to launch Europe's first startup accelerator dedicated exclusively to the sharing economy arena. We were surprised how may early-stage sharing economy startups were already trying to get a foothold in Europe and based in Barcelona. Early on we were contacted by the founders of several such startups, including Sharing Academy and Common Locals. We also were able to gain early support from city leaders in Barcelona as well as international thought-leaders such as Neal Gorenflo, founder of Shareable.net who I cited in Chapter 1, April Rinne, cited earlier in this chapter, leaders of Ouishare such as Albert Cañigueral and Antonin Leonard (co-founder of Ouishare) and Duncan McLaren, lead author of the 2016 book, Sharing Cities. We expect to support 5-10 Pan-European startups per year, while involving the City of Barcelona in the selection, mentoring, and yes, even the regulation of these responsible startups. The long-term vision is to support the creation of a network of such city-based accelerators in Europe and around the globe. Eventually, startups which are validated in Barcelona's accelerator could gain access to other cities through the network, and vice versa.

## CONCLUSION

In the twenty-first century, innovative cities are finding ways to attract and retain all forms of urban entrepreneurs and innovators. There is no simple formula because innovation is messy and, by nature, is constantly in flux. Cities can embrace tax policy and incentives, improve their governance and support through chief innovation officers, support the development of hard and soft infrastructure, and help to drive innovation opportunities for urban entrepreneurs through demand-side programs like civic crowdsourcing such as that offered by the BCN Open Challenge.

Speaking of Barcelona. One of the interviews I conducted in my research for this book was with Pere Condom, director of Programa Catalunya Emprèn ("Catalunya Startup"), who has been guiding the region's innovation and entrepreneurship policy for a few decades. He was involved in the beginning of 22@ and several other initiatives in Barcelona and the region, some of which have also been mentioned in this book. He is convinced that there are very few policy measures that can have a direct and immediate impact on the scale of the entrepreneurial ecosystem. Rather he recommends that policy makers take a long view of the investments they plan to make today. Many will pay off, like 22@ has for Barcelona, but most will take many years and sometimes even decades to have their full effect.

One last piece of advice for urban leaders and policy makers: when in doubt, get out of the way, because the drivers shaping urban entrepreneurship in modern cities are virtually impossible to hold back. Cities need to let urban tech, civic, and independent urban entrepreneurs take the lead.

# CHAPTER 6

## The Great Equalizer

*Boyd Cohen and Pablo Muñoz*

*The new direction of technological development should lead back to the actual size of man. Man is small, and, therefore, small is beautiful.*

—E.F. Schumacher (1973)

But in 2014, Minnesota must come to terms with a crisis unfolding across much of the state that will not attract the attention of the news choppers. This crisis is not threatening metro communities like Minneapolis or Eden Prairie. But to get a real feel for the crisis, take a long drive across Minnesota on rural highways such as U.S. 75, U.S. 212, MN 9 or MN 30. Make sure to tour small cities like Benson, Olivia, Tracy and Montevideo. Stop in smaller cities like Balaton, Ada, Hallock and Wheaton and have a cup of coffee. . . . what you may notice first in these communities is the number of empty storefronts and blank spaces on Main Street. The hardware store is gone. Maybe one cafe and one bar will still be open.[1]

This story of disappearing small towns is not just a U.S. phenomenon. Smaller towns and cities around the globe are struggling to stay relevant in today's hectic world. From small towns in China to rural regions in Portugal, the disappearing population and economic activity resulting from urbanization are placing a major strain, and in some cases resulting in the disappearance of smaller towns. With 2.5 billion people expected to move to cities by 2050, the question remains, what can be done about villages, small towns and cities, and rural areas that aspire to retain their heritage and perhaps even grow their populations, taking into account the trends Boyd laid out in this book?

Most of this book, the previous chapter included, has been biased toward larger cities, which makes sense since the great urban migration is already in place. Most urban migration is toward larger cities that have greater densities and more opportunities, and needs, for urban entrepreneurship. The larger cities are facing massive strains on their infrastructure, and their ability to provide equivalent, or improved, services to the growing masses is limited, requiring new ways of thinking and engagement with citizen and private sector innovators. However, in Boyd's speaking engagements throughout the world, he is frequently asked, what does all this mean for smaller towns and cities? Should they accept the inevitable exodus and pack up their tents, or is there something smaller towns and cities can do to stem the tide, or perhaps reverse it? Pablo has experienced a similar situation in developing his own work. How do we preserve local economies while promoting entrepreneurial behavior? Can we actually learn something from how small communities have overcome their circumstances through enterprising activities? This chapter is devoted to exploring what smaller communities can or are doing now to attract (or perhaps retain) the range of entrepreneurs discussed in this book.

## CHATTANOOGA, TENNESSEE

With a population of less than 200,000 and a legacy of industrial activity that, like most cities large and small, has declined substantially in recent decades, Chattanooga was facing an uphill battle to attract and retain young innovators. Yet, city leaders had other plans. They engaged in significant efforts at placemaking in the downtown area animating the riverfront with public spaces and parks, combined with private sector investment in new residential and commercial areas. The city dedicated a 140-acre section of the formerly industrial area of downtown Chattanooga for the creation of an innovation district. Spurred on by the creation of 9,000 miles of a high-speed fiber network (à la Kansas City and Barcelona), Chattanooga is making the most of its resources. Chattanooga has also embraced a critical component of the Urbanpreneur Spiral collaboration. According to Bruce Katz, a global expert from the Brookings Institution on innovation districts,

Chattanooga's innovation district is the product of genuine, enthusiastic collaboration—not often seen in bigger cities—between public, private, and civic institutions and leaders. These players include the city and county governments, EPB (the local energy utility) . . . the University of Tennessee at Chattanooga, The Enterprise Center and an entrepreneurial mix of investors like the Lamp

Post Group, start-ups like Bellhops, incubators like CO.LAB and real estate developers like River City Company, DEW Properties, and Fidelity Trust Company. I was continuously struck by the extent to which this diverse set of players—with very different experiences and world views—are truly "collaborating to compete" and grow something truly unique to their city. Something special is happening in Chattanooga. They are inventing a distinctive version of an innovation district that builds on their high quality of life, unique competitive advantages, and collaborative culture. The more traditional innovation districts have a lot to learn from the Gig City.[2]

## EMBRACING THE SHARING ECONOMY: SMALLER TOWNS, CITIES, AND SHARING REGIONS

At the end of 2014, Boyd was invited to keynote a smart cities event in Braganca, Portugal. We know what your first question is, "where is Braganca, Portugal and how could they possibly become a smart city?" Perhaps this is not the best place to admit it, but Boyd too had those questions when the speaking request came to him. He accepted the request because of the adventure and challenge of thinking about innovation and entrepreneurship in a range of contexts. Perhaps the offer of a 1961 bottle of Port wine from the region had something to do with his acceptance too.

He then went about studying what Braganca was all about. Boyd came to realize it was a rich agricultural region, with great scenery and part of Port wine country among other attractions. He also learned that they have experienced, like most smaller, rural regions, an exodus of the younger population who has migrated to the larger cities of Oporto and Lisbon in search of opportunity.

The more he thought about it, the more he came to believe that Braganca could make a name for itself by focusing on becoming a sharing region, encouraging sharing related start-ups and sharing tourism. There is a platform called helpx that connects travelers with working travel opportunities. Usually the traveler gains access to free lodging and boarding in return for 4 hours or so (per day) of service to the tourism operator. Boyd discovered in the Braganca region, Terra dos Sonhos, an aspiring ecotourism community offering housing and boarding in return for help in constructing their lodge. He also found dozens of Airbnb listings nearby, and in fact stayed in an Airbnb rental in Oporto on his way to Braganca. In his keynote address, Boyd suggested that communities like Braganca could combine shared access to coworking and 3D labs with initiatives to encourage working tourism. They could go further by developing cooperative renewable energy organizations and cooperative farms too. Now this sharing region approach may not sound like utopia to everyone, but we are willing to bet there are many young people in Portugal and around the world who would be attracted to this lifestyle.

Others are starting to think about the sharing region concept as well. Ouishare, one of the most important global organizations promoting the adoption of the sharing economy, has been working on the development of "sharitories," which

is a global project with a very practical scope: to create a Collaborative Territories Toolkit for local policy-makers around the world who wish to implement collaborative or sharing initiatives in their local areas and help them thrive.[3]

Much of their early work has focused on the idea of sharing regions as opposed to sharing only within major urban areas.

Kirklees, UK, provides another example of how smaller cities can differentiate themselves from the pack by embracing the sharing economy. In this book, Boyd has made a few references to the Bloomberg Foundation's efforts to support urban innovation through funding and human resource support. Kirklees, with a population of 430,000, proposed an ambitious program referred to as Kirklees Shares in the hopes of developing an inclusive and collaborative approach to sharing through government, civic, and private sector collaboration.

City governments everywhere face tightening constraints on resources alongside rising aspirations from ambitious citizens. Kirklees wants to stimulate and operate a new sharing economy to maximize untapped local resources and do more with less. The city will pool idle government assets—from vehicles, to venues, and citizens' skills and expertise—and work with the nonprofit sector to make these assets available through an online platform that will organize and allow for borrowing, bartering, and time-banking to benefit both programs and residents.[4]

Kirklees Shares is in its infancy, but the program objectives, if achieved, could have significant implications for the quality of life in the city and generate interesting opportunities for civic, indie, and even tech urban entrepreneurship.

## CINCINNATI: "FLY OVER NO MORE!"

Cincinnati is a small city of about 300,000 people in southern Ohio on the border with Kentucky and Indiana. Mostly known as the headquarters for Procter & Gamble, Kroger, and Macy's, Cincinnati does not have a reputation as a hot spot for the creative class. In fact, like many Midwestern cities, it used to be thought of as a city investors flew over on their trips between Silicon Valley and more vibrant East Coast cities such as Boston and New York.

Yet, things are changing fast for this city in the Midwest. Cincinnati now boasts one of the U.S. best start-up accelerators, the Brandery, a growing angel investment scene (Cincinnati's Queen City Angels are ranked second out of 370 angel organizations by CB Insights) and a handful of public-private partnerships geared toward accelerating the start-up scene.

In conducting research for this book, Boyd had the opportunity to speak with Kevin Mackey, offering product manager for Cincinnati-based Cintrifuse, who helped shed light on the evolution of the city in the past decade. Cintrifuse itself is a great example of an entity that emerged through the collaborative interests of government agencies, corporate leaders, and the start-up community.

Cintrifuse was formed after a group of visionary executives from major companies (as part of the Cincinnati Business Committee [CBC]) helped the city develop a long-term strategy to attract and retain innovators. Cintrifuse is dedicated to bridging the gaps between the public and private sectors, entrepreneurs, angel and venture capitalists, and corporate innovation needs with local and regional entrepreneurs. In fact, in collaboration with a state agency, Ohio Third Frontier Fund, major corporate partners like P&G and Duke Energy, and local universities such as the University of Cincinnati, Cintrifuse managed to develop a 57 million (USD) Syndicate Fund, which is used to entice venture capitalists looking to raise funds for investments in local start-ups.

Like start-up companies themselves, when venture capitalists are fundraising, they have to sell their case in person. So the Syndicate Fund solved the problem of "flyover country"—investors now have at least one major reason to come to Cincinnati. During their visits, Cintrifuse coordinates "Immersion Days"—meetings between VCs and start-ups, innovators within the big corporations, and other start-up organizations like The Brandery. The goal is to have them leave Cincinnati saying, "I had no idea how much is going on there!"

Perhaps one of the aspects of Cincinnati's growing success story that struck me was the role that the city's legacy, and sense of place, is being infused in the entrepreneurial community. Over the Rhine, one of Cincinnati's 52 neighborhoods, which was predominantly founded by German immigrants, was once largely a district for local breweries. Following a migration from local craft brews to national brands like

Budweiser and Miller, Over the Rhine fell on hard times. Recently, however, there has been a massive urban regeneration project in the past decade. Over the Rhine is now becoming a thriving hot spot for artists, innovators, and entrepreneurs to live and work. Cintrifuse is building a $16 million campus for innovation there. And rather than ditch their brewery history, the neighborhood is spawning a revival in craft breweries that are embracing the new entrepreneurial vibe in this part of the city. Rhinegeist, for example, took over a defunct brewery and launched a new brewery in 2013. Aside from making a range of locally crafted brews, Rhinegeist regularly hosts entrepreneurial events and other creative activities in the brewery.

Another interesting strategy being used by the city and ecosystem players such as Cintrifuse is to leverage the demand for new innovation needs by the handful of national and multinational firms that call Cincinnati home in order to encourage local and regional entrepreneurs to come to the city to pitch their solutions to the corporate challenges. Similar to civic crowdsourcing discussed in prior chapters, this approach (referred to as "Customer Connections") recognizes the entrepreneurial opportunities emerging from the needs of companies with a long history in the community and turns this into a magnet for attracting certain types of start-ups. The Brandery, for example, has a heavy focus on consumer-related technologies because of the connection to Procter & Gamble and Cincinnati's local cohort of consumer branding experts.

The mission of Cintrifuse is to build a great entrepreneurial ecosystem which is ultimately going to keep talent but as far as attracting talent, ("Customer Connections") is how we do that. If you are a startup and you sign a big deal with P&G, Kroger's or Macy's, these are billion dollar companies, you are probably going to set up an office here in Cincinnati . . . By leveraging the strength of these big corporations, we tell startups we can help you and we can offer you space and support here in Over the Rhine in Cincinnati.[5]

Many of you have probably heard the expression that it "takes a village to raise a child." This story from Cincinnati suggests that, perhaps particularly for smaller cities with less natural inertia and benefits that larger cities have, the same expression may apply. It takes a village to grow an entrepreneurial ecosystem! Cincinnati's emerging success has been the result of forward-thinking local officials (e.g., the mayor is on the board of Cintrifuse), committed corporate leaders (e.g., CBC), urban regeneration (e.g., Over the Rhine), connection to place (e.g., Customer Connections and the brewery district), and support organizations (e.g., the Brandery and Cintrifuse) to jump-start a local entrepreneurial ecosystem in smaller cities.

## WHAT IF THE SIZE IS EVEN SMALLER? TOWARD SHARING TOWNS

In July 2015, Pablo was involved in a rural entrepreneurship program in Puerto Saavedra, Chile, which, with the support of Balloon Chile, empowers more than 120 indigenous to become entrepreneurs. These families live in isolation in protected land with the nearest city about 100 miles away. Driving toward the area, there was a sign displaying "Urban Area," and right after another one with "Welcome to Puerto Dominguez, 11,400 inhabitants." The reflection is kind of obvious at this stage. How small a town or city is certainly depends on what we use as a point of comparison. Certainly, a city of 300,000 is small relative to the large metropolitan areas Boyd has discussed in the previous chapters. But what can we do when the size is even smaller? Can towns or villages 10 or 20 times smaller than Puerto Dominguez embrace the trends discussed in this book or, even more so, become a focal point for policy and practice?

We believe they can. Indeed, in our research we have found extraordinary cases of grassroots innovation that bring to life the principles of collaboration, democracy, sustainability, and entrepreneurship into the heart of socioeconomic community development.

From 2002 until 2006 Boyd was on the business faculty at the University of Victoria in Canada. One of his colleagues was Ana Maria Peredo, who has spent most of her academic career studying community-based entrepreneurship particularly in Latin America. In her widely cited 2006 paper in the *Academy of Management Review*, Peredo and her research colleague, James Chrisman, identified this emergent phenomenon as community-based entrepreneurship (CBE), which is defined as a community acting corporately as both entrepreneur and enterprise in pursuit of the common good. CBE is therefore the result of a process in which the community acts entrepreneurially, to create and operate a new enterprise embedded in its existing social structure.[6]

Community-based entrepreneurs typically band together to improve quality of life while producing a service or product for their communities. They are much like civic entrepreneurs in how they are frequently embedded in social and territorial systems. The main distinction we make between them is that usually CBE is associated with an organizational form of a cooperative with a collective group of community owners, whereas civic entrepreneurs commonly form independent enterprises but seek to collaborate with their communities where they operate, oftentimes through democratic business models. While CBE in some form or another has existed as long as communities have existed, Ana Maria and others sought to bring research attention to the process by which community members form such enterprises as well as highlighting the unique objectives most CBEs have.

Much of the research and discussion about CBEs has focused on communities in the base of the pyramid (BoP), but in recent years an increasing amount of attention has been paid to CBE's emergence in developed economies, since smart community enterprising has proven successful in the transition (and survival) of villages and towns.

In making sense of (urban) entrepreneurship in small towns, Pablo discovered a wonderful case of a 350-person community in the North of England who acted in the face of the 2008 financial crisis utilizing community enterprising and grassroots innovation.

## THE GEORGE AND DRAGON: FROM ABANDONED PUB TO SUSTAINABLE COMMUNITY ENTERPRISE

For more than 30 years the George and Dragon (G&D) had been the heart of the Hudswell Village, but the 2008 financial breakdown forced the pub out of business, together with more than 1,800 pubs around the country.

Everyone who has spent a week in England would know what pubs and pints mean and what this closure entails for the community. Not only it had lost the cultural resource of having a local pub, but also the everyday routines and practices related to work had been shattered together with the faith in the way of life they knew.

Although there was very little hope that someone would buy and reopen the G&D, the villagers refused to lose this emblematic place. One year later, a group of former pub regulars with 38 others made a formal community share offer of £209,950, risky move since they didn't have the money. Seems that the pub was worth it. Interestingly, the money didn't come from a traditional development agency, but from using their own version of civic crowdfunding, which raised more than £175,000 from over 150 community members and from other small pots across the region. As a result, anybody was welcomed to become an owner of the G&D through the community share scheme the group set up.

After reopening, the sales at the G&D have been consistently higher than anticipated, over 50 percent. Surprisingly, food- and family-oriented events (e.g., darts and dominoes competitions, book club, folk club, blues and country music night, quiz night, and the Women of Hudswell meetings) have been the main drivers for such sales growth. As the pub once was the beating heart of the Hudswell life, it provides not only a beer-centric meeting space but also a range of social, cultural, and sporting activities. The idea, however, was to go beyond the traditional community center. In order to do so, the community members needed to make the operations profitable, so they widened the scope of the venture to develop a range of new services and products.

## BEYOND THE PINTS AND PORK SCRATCHING

For the first time in more than 30 years, Hudswell residents got their own village shop. This G&D's spinoff is one of Hudswell's greatest achievements. Established with the help of grant aid from the York and North Yorkshire Community Foundation and the Big Lottery *Awards for All*, the "Little Shop" runs on 20 volunteers who take turns to work in two-hour shifts. The customers can access the shop while the pub is open, simply because it is located in a specially fitted room within the pub. Alongside produce, the shop provides a prescription collection service, a dry-cleaning service, and a parcel drop-off service.

Just like groceries, fresh vegetable and fruits also needed to travel long distances to get to the Hudswell's village. After reopening the pub and the shop, the community built 10 community allotments in the pub's backyard, and all of them were rented to villagers or members of Hudswell Community Pub. This represents not only an extra income for the community business but also a way of bringing the community closer, as the responsibility for supplying fresh vegetables and fruits now rests on the community's shoulders.

The G&D has also become a home for the Hudswell village library, being the first initiative of its kind in the country. This is one of a small but growing number of library services that are being moved into pubs as one solution to the deepening public libraries crisis, touched on in the last chapter. After moving the library to the pub, the number of readers has grown, and the community business is looking for ways to change the traditional library system in order to become less reliant on what the City Council has to offer to them. The aim is to improve the stock and keep it fresh. In order to do so, they have been borrowing ideas from the old and new sharing economy to pilot test a swap service, where people leave a book in return for a borrowed one. Reflecting on this experience, Martin Booth, secretary for the Hudswell Community Pub Initiative, says:

This is the kind of pro-active approach that is crucial if Yorkshire's rural communities are to enjoy a renaissance. Local enthusiasm and expertise can go a long way, as the residents of Hudswell are demonstrating with their venture that pools resources and brings key services together under one roof.

With the shop, allotments, library, and Internet access, community members feel that they have created a hub of services that make the G&D a real center of village activity and they have helped to create a more cohesive and friendly community in the village. Nowadays, nearly 50 firms and professionals and over 200 Hudswell community members keep the business running. All 200 people share the ownership of the venue and can use it to organize local events and celebrations. Looking ahead, the community pub plans to grow the business to provide bed and breakfast accommodation in the near future. Local volunteers already started exploring the hospitality business by building new hiking trails from and back to the pub.

## WHY BOTHER?

In giving new life to the pub, community members got involved in improving the infrastructure. The costs of refurbishment were considerably lower than they might have been, due to the voluntary effort that was donated by Hudswell Community Pub members and by other villagers and supporters. Most contractors were local tradesman and many local firms donated the supplies and equipment needed. All this was a genuine community effort. The board set a buy-to-rent model, so Margaret and Jackie Stubbs took over the G&D pub rights, but out of the entire population of Hudswell (353 people), 170 were HCP members (at the time of refurbishment). Finally, on the June, 12, 2011, the Hudswell Community reopened the pub to once again serve as the real center for village life.

The process of acquiring and opening the pub demonstrated how something that originally seemed inconceivable was made possible by changing assumptions on who can be an entrepreneur and by establishing a hybrid organization that uses entrepreneurship as a means to support community life. Instead of getting passivized and struggling with unemployment, the community members came together to work for the common good.

Small, urban enterprising emerges by articulating grassroots, inclusive innovation that needs no clear organizational structure. Authority and labor was effectively distributed, enabling joint decision-making for commonly defined goals. The community's previously scattered financial possessions were collected and practical skills were utilized for buying and refurbishing the pub—thus turning the existing and latent resources into a useful and productive base for the entrepreneurial operations.

## SMART COMMUNITIES AND ENTREPRENEURSHIP

Not only can CBEs develop innovative solutions for food and pubs, but they can also be used to provide more complex solutions to communities. Communities around the globe, for example, have banded together to form energy cooperatives focused on obtaining and delivering renewable energy to their homes and businesses. In his 2011 book *Climate Capitalism*, Boyd and his coauthor Hunter Lovins highlighted Denmark's Samsø Island as a fascinating example of energy-based CBEs. Somsø Island, with a population of only 3,800, has had a long-term commitment to sustainable development including organic farming and free-range animal production. In 1997, the island won a Danish government competition to develop and implement a strategy to become a 100 percent renewable energy island. However, the plan from the beginning was to embrace the community in the energy transformation. Therefore, the project was conceived as an energy cooperative whereby every resident is a co-owner of the 10 wind turbines.

Denmark has a long tradition of cooperatives, the accepted mechanism to raise funds to build and run community facilities. As member-owners, Samsøers enjoy low heating costs, thanks to district heating systems they collectively own, while their shares generate annual dividend checks based on each wind turbine's output and the going price of electricity. The more energy efficient a coop member's farm, the greater his net earnings. And by producing more renewable energy than it consumes, the island's net carbon emission is zero.[7] Today, the island supplies 100 percent of its electricity needs through wind power and actually generates excess capacity, which is sold to mainland Denmark.

## ISLE OF EIGG

Another island in the northwest of Scotland is also taking the lead in zero emissions, zero waste, and energy efficiency through collaboration and community enterprising. The Isle of Eigg is an 87-person village that nearly 20 years ago decided to buy, protect, and develop the island by creating the Heritage Trust. The trust's mission was far from revolutionary, but its approach certainly was. Instead of just worrying about job creation or the conservation of natural habitats, the trust was established to provide and create opportunity for economic development, housing, and infrastructure, while conserving the natural and cultural heritage to ensure that development takes place in a sustainable way. In 2009, most of the island's 38 households got involved in Nesta's Big Green Challenge project, which aimed at learning from selected communities in Britain while reducing their carbon footprint. By fostering entrepreneurial behavior, the community developed a wide range of projects, from generating renewable electricity to collectively producing their own food. In January 2010, the Eigg community won joint first place in Nesta's competition (and £300,000) because they found new and better ways to tackle climate change. Currently Eigg generates virtually 100 percent of its electricity using renewable energy produced by a combination of a 10 kW hydroelectric generator, two smaller hydro electric generators of 10 kW and 9 kW, four 6 kW wind generators, and 30 kW of solar electric cells, which is remarkable for a low-tech, 87-person community living an hour away from Mallaig and Arisaig, by ferry. This entrepreneurial community certainly has something to feel proud about and could inspire others to do the same.

The Isle of Eigg has exceeded our expectations of what communities can achieve in reducing carbon emissions and for this they should be congratulated. The success of the project proves that, when communities are incentivized, empowered and supported, they become a compelling force in solving some of society's biggest challenges.[8]

## ATTRACTING CIVIC ENTREPRENEURS

Similarly, towns and cities can embrace engagement of citizens in urban regeneration programs. From a 2015 blog post in Urbact:

Bottom-up regeneration, similar to community-led or participative regeneration, is revitalization and renovation of a public space initiated by the local community or local NGOs. Often it is connected to temporary use of empty premises or abandoned building sites until those get another purpose. One of such building sites in Ljubljana got a new life when a local NGO decided to use it for urban gardening. Similar happened in Tobačna factory, where the local creative milieu established a coworking space. In Ljubljana, there are two very successful bottom-up regeneration projects—Park Tabor and Savsko naselje, both initiated by a local NGO.[9]

Incorporate the concept of the city as a lab and smaller cities could find ways to encourage civic entrepreneurs to utilize their own infrastructure as a test bed for their prototyped concepts. Pilot projects in a small town can be much faster to implement and allow for a controlled experiment that doesn't run the risk of affecting millions of daily commuters, for example. Citymart.com is a platform that connects civic innovators with cities in need of innovative solutions around the globe. A civic entrepreneur could test their solution in their small town, upload their results on Citymart, and market their services to small and large services around the globe.

## ATTRACTING INDIE URBANPRENEURS

We believe there is an opportunity for smaller towns and cities to succeed in attracting and retaining the creative class by embracing indie urbanpreneurs. The invisible infrastructure discussed in the indie urbanpreneur chapter does not have to be that expensive. Think back to Ryan Gepper and his Coolest Cooler campaign. Yes, he lives in San Diego, a relatively larger city. But what did he need to be successful? Internet access, ideally a 3D prototyping facility, and the idea. Why do those things need to be available only in larger cities? A smaller town or city could also fund the creation of coworking spaces and shared 3D labs and build a brand for itself as the place for indie urbanpreneurs to come, live more inexpensively, and prototype their ideas. Of course another key ingredient for many of these indie urbanpreneurs is the networking assets that are frequently more robust in larger cities. If a smaller city wanted to become a magnate for indie urbanpreneurs, it could work to create the enabling conditions to attract a diverse array of artists, innovators, makers, and others to create a small but active ecosystem and perhaps adapt the sister city concept by finding ways to connect the local indie urbanpreneurs with those from other small towns in the region or beyond.

Recall in Chapter 4, Boyd wrote about the emergence of several platforms that contribute to the growth of the on-demand economy where individuals bid for projects from other individuals or companies in their same city (e.g., TaskRabbit) or around the globe (e.g., Elance). Stack Overflow is another such service connecting programmers and developers with projects from start-ups and companies around the globe. In 2015 they conducted a developer survey with more than 28,000 responses from 157 countries. Among the survey questions related to the location of the developers when conducting their work. Surprisingly, they found that developers who worked remotely made higher salaries than those who worked at the client site.[10] While there could be numerous explanations for this finding, the point is that it could be possible for a smaller town or city to create a hub of on-demand independent workers who could deliver programming services remotely. Remember the story of Kansas City implementing Google Fiber? Smaller communities doing something similar could attract such programmers seeking a more peaceful life and most likely one where their income would stretch much further. Implementing broadband infrastructure in a smaller town or city the size of Chattanooga is much cheaper than in a megacity!

## ARTISANS AND MAKERS

The Etsy platform (discussed in Chapter 4) connects artisans and makers to global consumers. Rural areas and smaller cities often have a higher proportion of artisan types than do cities, given that the draw of cities is often toward employment in companies or start-ups. Artisans often have a strong social and territorial identity associated with where they live and they leverage local materials for making their wares. Before the advent of the Internet and platforms like Etsy, such artisans were quite limited in finding customers by depending on physical retail locations or stalls in their communities. But digital, two-sided markets like Etsy provide a new avenue for these independent entrepreneurs to reach a larger market while remaining in their community, which has shaped and inspired their artistry.

Rockford, Illinois, with a population of 150,000 has been facing serious economic decline coupled with increased crime resulting from their dwindling manufacturing base. Not content to see the town fall further into decline, their mayor, Larry Morrissey, reached out to Etsy to explore partnerships for educating future makers. This outreach inspired the creation of Etsy's Craft Entrepreneurship program. Etsy and the Rockford Housing Authority entered into a partnership to create a four-week training program to participants to turn their arts and crafts hobbies into something they can market via Etsy's platform.

But there's a part of Etsy's ethos that most don't talk about: its commitment to helping struggling cities foster local entrepreneurs.[11]

This Craft Entrepreneurship program suggests that Etsy is also playing the role of a global, platform-style civic entrepreneur. By committing to supporting struggling towns and cities with training programs for aspiring artisans, Etsy is contributing to local community building and economic development. Now, we would not say that this initiative is for altruistic purposes since it is of course in Etsy's business interests to grow the user and seller base.

## URBAN TECH ENTREPRENEURS IN SMALLER TOWNS

Now this one is a bit trickier. The allure of bigger cities for the urban tech entrepreneur makes it difficult for small towns to compete for such innovators. Yet, surprisingly, the data suggest that smaller cities and towns are still important generators of new technology innovation. Researchers from Waterloo (Canada) and Stanford recently analyzed the home base for people who had applied for patents between 1836 and 2010. They actually found that in recent decades, the percentage of patent filers living in dense urban environments is actually on the decline.

Our empirical findings indicate that during the 20th century inventions in large US cities built on recent advances much more often than comparable inventions in smaller US cities. The findings also indicate that during the most recent decades this advantage of large cities has waned. The advantage of locating R&D resources in large cities over locating the same resources in smaller cities thus seems to be much smaller now than it has been in the past.[12]

Of course in earlier chapters of this book, Boyd sought to demonstrate that the democratization of technology and open innovation were challenging the paradigm that patents are the best metric of modern innovation. We still feel that way, but the aforementioned research does suggest that some smaller towns and cities are able to attract certain types of innovators who could generate technology innovations that are relevant on a regional or even a global scale.

# CHAPTER 7

## Challenges of and Reflections on the Future of Urbanpreneurship

*Boyd Cohen and Pablo Muñoz*

We have made many claims throughout this book regarding the implications of the three converging factors that make up the Urbanpreneur Spiral: collaborative, urbanized, and democratized. We have also painted a generally rosy picture about life (rather naïve some may argue) and opportunities in cities. Yet we are quite aware of the challenges facing our cities, especially because of the great urban migration discussed in Chapter 2. In this chapter we aim to discuss some of the challenges facing modern cities and how urbanpreneurship may, in some cases, exacerbate them. We will then reflect on where all this might go in the future and the implications of this for individuals, cities, and society.

Let's start with some of the criticisms. One of the main drawbacks of promoting social and economic development has been and still is gentrification, which results from the arrival of wealthier people in an existing urban district and the subsequent increment in rents and property values, which changes the district's culture and social life. Likewise, and sometimes as a result of gentrification, further exclusion is created when affluence leads to social dislocation by buying locals out of the district. Gentrification and exclusion are critical matters. The *Guardian*[1] even has an online special section on it. So far, not so good news for the rise of urbanpreneurship arena. There is a third critique we need to address carefully, since it relates directly to our model, namely, market stability and labor. We already tackled some criticisms from the neoliberal crowd in a previous chapter. Nothing wrong with them sticking to their ideas; in the end, the sharing economy seems to resonate too much with socialist ideals, but there are gray areas that need to be factored into the urbanpreneurship equation.

## DOES THE INFUSION OF URBANPRENEURS EXACERBATE SOCIAL ILLS IN CITIES?

Yes urbanpreneurs can help improve the local economy, grow jobs in the city, drive investment in local infrastructure, and increase the number of housing units. But this may not always be good, especially for all citizens. One of the biggest and most persistent critiques of frameworks toward innovation districts and the creative class, and Richard Florida's work in particular, has been the suggestion that attracting new innovators into urban areas has the tendency to result in social exclusion and displacement of lower-income residents. Urban policy scholars have been particularly interested in understanding what types of actions cities take to embrace the creative class and what implications these policies have on local communities. Catungal et al. studied the Liberty Village initiative in Toronto and concluded that "the failure of creative city initiatives to forge truly open and creative spaces raises questions about how mutually supportive relationships between art, culture and local communities might be forged."[2]

Atkinson and Easthope studied the impact of creative class strategies in five Australian cities. "We find that the rhetoric of universal social potential accompanying creative city ideas continues to overlook those unable to participate in this new economy, as well as those who are more actively excluded."[3] Urban renewal, or arguably gentrification and displacement, in Washington, D.C., have been under way for decades now. Professor Charles Hostovsky recently noted that the percentage of African Americans in D.C. has declined from 77 percent in 1970 to 49 percent in 2014.[4]

Having listened to the ongoing criticism associated with cities seeking to attract the creative class and the assumed negative repercussions for lower-income, less-educated urban residents, Richard Florida, in his latest book *The New Urban Crisis*, takes on this criticism head-on. Florida recognizes that increasingly superstar cities such as New York, Tokyo, Hong Kong, and Paris are becoming havens for the 1 percent and pricing out the other 99 percent. Florida refers to this tendency as "winner-take-all urbanism." Florida states:

The process of gentrification is surely wrenching, difficult, and traumatic for the people it displaces, but much of the dialogue about it is not only disingenuous, it distracts from an even more serious urban problem, which is neighborhoods that stay poor. A growing number of social scientists have concluded that the very construct of gentrification is vague and ideologically loaded.[5]

Despite recognizing the oftentimes detrimental impacts of gentrification from the creative class migration, Florida then focuses much of his attention on the larger problem of permanently poor neighborhoods that have not been bettered by the infusion of innovators and associated improvements to the urban form.

Here we would like to address, albeit briefly, the challenge of how modern cities can increasingly attract educated innovators without displacing the core of what made the city attractive in the first place.

## IS THE SHARING ECONOMY REALLY GOOD FOR CITIES AND CITIZENS?

One of the key drivers discussed throughout this book is the promise of collaborative business models and, in particular, the sharing economy for urban innovation and urbanpreneurs. We believe the potential the sharing economy poses for positive impacts in areas ranging from economic opportunity, climate change, and social inclusion is significant. Yet we are really only in the very nascent stage of the sharing economy revolution and there is insufficient data to understand what its impacts already are, let alone what they could be in the future. While most of this book treated the sharing economy as a positive contributor to the growth of urbanpreneurship, here we would like to reflect on many of the valid concerns emerging about this form of economic activity. Ultimately, there is an unavoidable reality: the sharing economy does have an impact on social inclusion.

Not only can urban renewal or gentrification lead to displacement of local and lower-income residents, so too can the sharing economy. Cities around the globe, including Barcelona, where Boyd currently resides, have launched an assault on Airbnb and other similar short-term tourist rental services. The primary reason: the acquisition and rental of entire apartment units and, in some extreme cases, entire apartment buildings for Airbnb short-term rentals results in a decreased housing stock for local residents. Furthermore, as buildings and neighborhoods become repurposed for tourists, the availability of services for residents dwindles. Where before there may have been local hardware stores, grocery stores, and drycleaners, commercial areas transform to liquor stores and tacky tourist souvenir shops, decreasing the quality of life for locals and eroding the neighborhood's historic character, ironically making the same neighborhoods less attractive to the cultured tourist. Barceloneta, an area of intense tourism activity adjacent to Barcelona's beach and, not so coincidentally, the port for cruise ships, has been hit hardest by the Airbnb phenomenon.

As anecdotal evidence, Boyd conducted a search for a place in the Barceloneta neighborhood for May 2016 for two people and discovered 294 available rentals, 192 of which were for the entire apartment. The volume of tourists flooding Barceloneta, and the growing number of Airbnb units in the neighborhood, led locals to lodge more than 200 complaints to the neighborhood association and to host several protests against tourists in the streets. Recently the city has banned the issuance of new permits for individuals seeking to rent their units in full or in part to tourists. Of course Barcelona is not alone in its concern about the potential negative implications of the explosion of Airbnb. Cities like New York, Berlin, and Portland, Oregon, have all had their battles with Airbnb, although the latter entered into an agreement with Airbnb to implement more regulatory controls.

Even while recognizing the potential downsides of sharing such as that offered by Airbnb, the jury is really still out on the net affect these business models have as they scale. In its own defense, Airbnb conducted research on the 4,000 hosts in Barcelona and discovered, for what it's worth, that 75 percent of hosts had income levels at or below the national average, suggesting that the additional revenue from hosting visitors allows locals to subsidize their mortgage or rent, essentially making housing more affordable.[6]

## ON-DEMAND ECONOMY'S IMPACT ON THE WORKFORCE

Many other platforms in the sharing economy space have also raised significant concern. The on-demand economy, or gig economy, which was discussed at length in our Chapter 4 on indie urbanpreneurs, is also generating significant controversy. Companies like TaskRabbit, Handy, and Uber (although we don't actually consider most of Uber's activities to actually be part of the sharing economy—their primary business model is a private taxi fleet, there is no sharing going on) facilitate short-term freelance work connecting people in need of a service with individuals willing to perform that service on a piecemeal basis. One could argue these services have the potential to increase efficiency in the marketplace and actually generate independent work for people who perhaps otherwise would be unemployed. Yet many economists, politicians, and on-demand workers have claimed these platforms exploit freelancers, leaving them with no pension, no unemployment benefits, and usually without health care and other benefits associated with full-time employment.

The so-called on-demand economy looks here to stay, however, so we need to think more as a society, and at a country and city level, how we want to regulate these new marketplaces. Many countries like Japan, the United States, and most of Europe as well are aging and not replacing their aging population. Social security to the aging is dependent on revenues from the current workforce paying into social security. What will happen to social security systems, pension schemes, and the like as a growing percentage of the population, even professionals like lawyers, doctors, and consultants, actively participate in the on-demand economy?

## WHAT CAN WE DO TODAY?

We can't run away from criticisms since they are, as mentioned, unavoidable realities. We can't confront them, since, although we appreciate the benefits of the sharing economy and the urbanpreneurship phenomenon, we are academics first and foremost and not advocates of the concept, neither lobbyists for that matter. We can't ignore them either because there are people involved, and if our propositions are to impact decision-makers—we will keep our fingers crossed—we need them to be aware of the pros, cons, and challenges this phenomenon poses to urban entrepreneurial ecosystems and to quality of life in our cities. What we can do though is shed light on some emerging trends and thoughts around how to move this forward (carefully) while avoiding the unintended, and sometimes nasty, consequences.

## GENTRIFICATION WITHOUT DISPLACEMENT

So the billion-dollar question is can cities continue to attract innovators and urbanpreneurs through some form of urban renewal of decaying neighborhoods (à la Barcelona's initiative with the 22@ innovation district) without creating displacement of the bohemian culture and lower-income residents who helped make the city or neighborhood attractive for innovators in the first place? Earlier in the book Boyd discussed the Medellín approach to urban renewal. We believe looking at the Medellín case helps provide insight into how it is possible to attract more urbanpreneurs and raise the quality of life for lower-income residents without displacing them.

Medellín was the crime-infested base of operations for one of the most violent and dominant drug lords of the twentieth century, Pablo Escobar. While Escobar reinvested some of his ill-gotten profits in civic amenities like schools and soccer fields, they were completed with the ulterior motive of gaining more control and protection from local residents. From the 1970s to the early 1990s, Escobar's band wreaked havoc on Medellín, turning the city into a war zone. Escobar and his hitmen are "credited" with the murder of thousands of people, including hundreds of police; dozens of bombings, including of a plane in 1989; and several political kidnappings.[7] Besides violent crime, Medellín struggled with the growth of informal settlements in the outskirts of the city housing the city's poor in substandard conditions, quite similar in many respects to the favelas of Rio.

In the mid-2000s however, Medellín's mayor, Sergio Fajardo, embarked on a path of urban regeneration with a goal of making Medellín a safer city while improving the local economy and attracting more innovators to the city. Fajardo implemented a strategy focused on improving the quality of life for low-income residents, including better education, attacking youth unemployment, and perhaps, most importantly, significant investments in infrastructure such as libraries and transportation for lower-income residents. The strategy has been transformative and has set Medellín up to be a global leader in urban renewal with the "rising tide lifts all boats" approach. Rather than provide incremental improvements to transport and facilities, Fajardo and his successors have chosen to build up pride in the lower-income neighborhoods by implementing innovative transportation schemes such as the Metrocable and outdoor escalators designed to connect the poor neighborhoods in the outskirts to economic, educational, and social opportunities in the city. The city also attracted investment into projects like Library Parks, which includes one of Colombia's most attractive and expensive libraries, Biblioteca España, in one of the city's, and the country's for that matter, poorest neighborhoods. In only a few years, Medellín was radically transformed, experiencing a massive reduction in the homicide rate of 90 percent.[8]

Yet, as discussed in previous chapters, the Medellín story doesn't end there. While the poor neighborhoods have experienced sizeable increases in quality infrastructure and services, the local residents are not being displaced by the "White Millennials" as is the case in D.C. Rather lower-income residents are increasingly connected and educated and being invited to participate in the creative economy, which is flourishing in the city. The Ruta N innovation district is attracting urbanpreneurs from around the country and the Latin American region. Increasingly, residents from the poorer communities are able to participate in the innovation economy through STEM education initiatives and, of course, through better transit connections to the innovation hubs in the city.

Another interesting example of a city seeking to engage in urban renewal in an approach that results in inclusion, rather than exclusion, of lower-income residents is Vancouver. As a cofounder of the green building consultancy, Recollective, Boyd had the opportunity to live and work in Vancouver and Vancouver Island for 11 years. During his time there, Boyd was invited to join a consulting team working on the Vancouver Athletes' Village. The Athletes' Village, located in Southeast False Creek, a stone's throw from downtown Vancouver, was previously an industrial area bordering the Creek, a tributary of the Pacific Ocean. The land had become toxic and the buildings had gone into disrepair.

The City of Vancouver recognized this 7-hectare site had serious potential given its proximity to the downtown core, access to existing transit corridors, and the appeal of the adjacent creek. Over a 10-year period, the city managed to work with planners, consultants, and citizens to rethink this space in a postindustrial Vancouver. Through a competitive bidding process, the city encouraged developers to propose a massive rebuild into a green, live-work community that would first be used to house athletes for the 2010 winter Olympics. A key requirement for the winning developer was to ensure sufficient affordable housing would be included in the development. In return for including affordable housing, the city offered the winning developer the opportunity to construct more market-rate units on the site beyond what the current zoning laws would have dictated. This density bonus, therefore, was included to enable the winning developer to generate more revenue from high-end property (many of which sold for $1 million or more) to subsidize the construction of affordable housing units. Of the 1,100 units constructed, 250 were classified as affordable housing and 100 were "modest housing" with subsidies.[9] While the eventual developer experienced many financial difficulties on this project (some of which can be attributed to the global recession), we can point to the Vancouver Athletes' Village project as one that focused on attracting the creative class and lower-income residents into the same project.

## CAN THE SHARING ECONOMY BE PART OF THE SOLUTION?

Aside from the astronomical valuations of major sharing economy players like Airbnb (or exits in the case of Zipcar), there is still room for optimism that not only does the sharing economy pose major economic opportunity for dominant players, it also has the potential to improve the lives of everyday people. A modeling exercise recently completed by two scholars at NYU, for example, finds that eventual, peer-to-peer sharing will allow "below-median income consumers (to) enjoy a disproportionate fraction of eventual welfare gains from this kind of 'sharing economy' through broader inclusion, higher quality rental-based consumption, and new ownership facilitated by rental supply revenues."[10]

While today it appears the sharing economy has been more directed toward middle and upper income earners who are more digitally connected and increasingly urban, their research suggests that over time, the promise of access over ownership will have great appeal to lower and middle income people (who will increasingly cross the digital divide) and will benefit more from the incremental revenue from renting out something they do not need on a daily basis and saving money by doing the reverse. The sharing economy, therefore, has the potential to allow for more inclusion and raise the standard of living for all. Whether or not that actually happens will depend on a whole host of variables including: which business models emerge and scale, closing the digital divide, and how local and national governments address and regulate the sharing economy. Some local governments have already started moving in this direction, supporting those who truly offer and make use of underutilized resources, and banning those who only see here, as the famed economist Hayek would put it, purely opportunities for profit.

On the other hand, the sharing economy goes well beyond tech-based sharing platforms, covering a wide range of not-so-upscale urban areas, such as slums and favelas. Sharing economy, if seen through the lens of collective lending frequently used in microfinance, holds great promise for higher financial inclusion in lower-income areas. It is still debatable whether creating markets for the poor is the way forward if the aim is solving deep needs, yet we see tremendous opportunities for low-income urbanpreneurs and alternative finance mechanisms, which can creatively put together solutions for micro-entrepreneurs beyond what they currently do for the crowdfunded start-up nation. This will also force an updating of the traditional financial institutions if they are to play a role in this emerging sector. April Rinne in an article in the *Huffington Post* reflected on this matter already:

The sharing economy will not solve today's global economic woes, no more than microfinance can (not) single-handedly solve global poverty alleviation. But it is a powerful and helpful option to have that did not exist before, and should be promoted as such.[11]

## SHARING JOBS

For a traditional mindset, job security and long-term commitments are certainly big things, and having come to this world in the 1970s we are trapped in a similar mindset, through our efforts to join the movement. They show determination, mental stability and give the sense of "feet on the ground" when it comes to difficult decisions. On the contrary, a CV showing 20 part-time jobs, 10 projects (5 of which failed), and 2 ongoing volunteering jobs in the last 2 years is just the wrong way to start a career. A conservative advisor would argue that this one is doomed already. Millennials, who are key players in the urbanpreneurship universe, have proven that this might not be the case. It all depends on expectations and what a job actually means. Many historical jobs lacked a sense of purpose, and this is what many millennials are looking for. They commit to purpose, not to a corporate ladder.

If seen through the lens of income tax and pension schemes, this is a massive disaster. Social security relies on it, and we have a generation basically worried about this, not clear on what is the next move for them. Work for a year "on-demand" to travel to the next gig might be nonsense for Robert Reich, because under the economist mantra this affects jobs security, wages, and subsequently equality. It is not that the sharing generation is not worried about it. As we see it, first, the rules of the game are just not in the right place, and second, there might be different ways of building collective security and equality. The sharing, on-demand economy might be actually a more efficient way to do so.

This generation might be right after all, especially in light of the aftermath of the recent economic downturns in the United States and Europe, where, for example, almost 50 percent of the recent graduates in Spain are unemployed due to real estate gamblers and greed at home and across the Atlantic. As we have seen by the Great Recession, large corporations and banks are not always reliable sources of steady employment, let alone employment growth.

What if there are no viable job prospects for some individuals regardless of education levels? What if being an urbanpreneur is an alternative to being unemployed? Unemployment brings all kinds of other social problems including lack of self-esteem, increased crime, and dependence on the government (local, regional, and national) with respect to food and shelter. Granted some urbanpreneurs will choose to be so in lieu of viable job options. But is that necessarily a bad thing? That leaves jobs available to people who want them while allowing for enterprising individuals to leverage their ingenuity and initiative, and perhaps access to invisible infrastructure, the opportunity to earn a living (or occasionally much more than that) on their own terms.

## HYPE, DIVERSITY OR HERE TO STAY?

One final concern relates to how deep and actually transformational is the phenomenon we are referring to. Is it actually new, or the rebranding of an old practice? Is it a trend that will eventually succumb to the capitalist rules? Is it here to stay and will it change the entire system? Or is it simply an alternative form that adds more diversity to an already diversified economy? As we already stated in a recent paper,[12] we do not know the answer to those questions, and would argue no one does yet. However, it is possible to consider what lasting impact the sharing economy may have already had on economies and society.

The introduction of new business models and economic approaches such as the sharing economy activities discussed herein, have already created new, and often conflicting narratives amongst numerous stakeholders with respect to the benefits and drawbacks of sharing activity, appropriate regulatory approaches and varying rates of resistance and adoption from industry incumbents and peer groups in territories around the globe. These narratives represent different interpretations about what the sharing economy is, what it can and can't do. The mere existence of sharing economy activities has opened up the field allowing for interpretative flexibility. From this perspective, the sharing economy has already had a lasting impact on society in the sense that it has helped generate meaningful discussion regarding the role of the economy in society, peer to peer business models and alternatives to traditional capitalism.[13]

We (Boyd and Pablo) have discussed this several times, arriving to the conclusion we highlight above, but it is possible this was not an economic phenomenon in the first place and we got it all wrong. Looking backward to moving forward, we may realize that we might be dealing with a remake of *Back to the Future*.

Many in the sharing economy space are quick to point out that in fact sharing is not really new. Bartering, historically in rural and indigenous communities, has existed for centuries. Albeit in those days sharing was not aided by technology platforms that limited their reach, but also ensured a level of trust because you were one or at most two degrees of separation from the person you were sharing an object with. Yet there are tech-based and non-tech-based sharing platforms that are gaining traction in cities around the globe. A few years ago, a Repair Café was formed in Amsterdam with the goal of building community and enabling an environment for locals to bring their broken objects stored somewhere in their house to a café environment whereby someone with skills to repair stuff would do so, without charge. You might think that in the generally ego-driven society of many fast-paced cities, there would be little uptake on such a hippy, back to the 1960s type idea. Think again. Today there are more than 800 Repair Cafés around the globe, including one in Santiago, Chile, which Pablo founded along with his wife, Carolina, in 2014, before moving back to the UK.

Bliive, is a São Paulo, Brazil-based platform for connecting providers of services with those seeking services. On the surface this sounds just like the on-demand economy start-ups discussed above. Think again. No cash changes hands in the Bliive community. Instead of services in exchange for a fee, service providers receive "Time Money," which can be exchanged for services from other providers using the site. Bliive has a global provider base, offering more than 90,000 services![14]

## WHAT MIGHT COME NEXT

First off, we are not in the business of soothsaying and no one can, for certain, predict how all this will play out in cities of the future, or how the Urbanpreneur Spiral will look like 50 years on. Yet our current research and observations lead us to take a leap and make some assertions about where innovation and entrepreneurship in urban areas will go in the coming decades. Here we will talk about implications for entrepreneurs, cities, and society of the Urbanpreneur Spiral, the different emerging forms of urbanpreneurship and initiatives from cities, both large and small, discussed in the previous chapters. In 10 years feel free to share with us all the flawed assumptions and predictions we made here.

## THE FUTURE OF URBANPRENEURS

The Great Urban Migration will continue through 2100, with most of the additional population in developing countries of Africa and Asia. It is not a surprise, following this trend, that cities will be increasingly challenged to provide the basic infrastructure, services, housing, and jobs to meet the needs, and expectations of their growing masses. Urbanpreneurs will become much more important going forward, as cities will be desperate for alternative approaches and business models to complement city services. This of course will continue to raise concerns about too much private sector involvement in city administration.

We believe we will continue to see a decreasing dependence on venture capital to fund earlier stages of start-up development. Only the largest, most scalable start-ups will obtain venture capital. Instead we will see more of an explosion in the use of crowdfunding, lean start-up strategies and bootstrapping entrepreneurs across all spectrums of urbanpreneurship discussed here. We also suspect we will see a lot of hybrid urbanpreneurs who combine on-demand project work with on-the-side, start-up activity, leveraging a growing number of coworking spaces and 3D/Fab Labs. In this way, urbanpreneurs can maintain an income from on-demand projects, but keep the flexibility to tinker. Trends in the democratization of innovation discussed throughout this book suggest that the cost of prototyping new ideas and posting them on crowdfunding platforms means that there is little risk for such hybrid activity from urbanpreneurs. As demand increases for an innovation, a hybrid urbanpreneur will be able to allocate more time to their enterprise and less time to on-demand projects.

Another potential area of future development in this space is the convergence of different forms of urbanpreneuring. Boyd touched on this in Chapter 3 by showing how the urban tech movement has been overlapping with the civic entrepreneurship space leading to the emergence of civic tech. Another such overlap is starting to emerge between the civic entrepreneur and the maker movement (i.e., the indie urbanpreneur). Why couldn't makers apply their skills in crafting innovations toward the challenges in the neighborhoods and cities? The Research Director for the Institute for the Future, John Tester, recently observed the power of this intersection:

Civic hacking is a spirit that the city is a platform to remix ideas and data, to build DIY solutions, to tinker with existing systems and improve life for people—a spirit that the city is open for anyone to experiment. Makers, artists, coders, civic hackers, and citizens across the world have quickly adopted this mindset and joined this movement, and civic hacking has become a foundation for more open, more participatory cities.[15]

## THE FUTURE OF INNOVATIVE CITIES

Cities will hopefully accelerate the use of procurement for innovation, using an increasingly higher percentage of their budgets on finding more innovative solutions to their most pressing problems. We also expect, or at least hope, that cities will embrace open-source strategies and global, or at least regional, standards for the application of technologies for sensors, open data, and the like, which will allow for more scalable solutions by civic tech entrepreneurs.

## U.S. WILL LOSE ITS POSITION AS THE GLOBAL INNOVATION POWERHOUSE (AND NOT BECAUSE OF CHINA)

We believe that we are going to see a diffusion of innovation capability around the globe. The U.S. economy is resilient and has proven successful in overcoming crises, arguably because of its entrepreneurial spirit, yet we do not believe that it will retain its position as the global capital of entrepreneurship and innovation. The United States has historically been viewed as the most innovative and entrepreneurial country in the world. Most of the world's largest multinationals were founded in the United States and the United States has long been home to the largest venture capital market, with nearly $50 billion in venture capital investments in 2014,[16] and of course, to the icon of entrepreneurship and innovation, Silicon Valley.

As discussed earlier in this book, however, the importance of venture capital and suburban tech parks seems to be in decline. Open innovation, two-sided platforms, crowdfunding, and urban innovation seem to be driving much of the current innovation and entrepreneurship scenes around the globe. Away from the venture capital–intensive economy, countries in Northern Europe are exploring different forms of incentivizing citizen-focused platforms for collaborative decision-making and collective innovation. A EU-based study[17] highlights recent developments that support our arguments. While Iceland is planning to produce the first wiki-constitution, the Finnish government has set up an experiment called the Open Ministry to test crowdsourcing legislation.

These and other initiatives are being promoted by the EU D-CENT project, which stands for Decentralized Citizens Engagement Technologies. D-CENT seeks to develop the next generation of open-source tools for direct democracy and economic empowerment.

D-CENT surely resonates with another cool EU-based project: CO-Mantova. This is a prototype of a process to run the city as a collaborative commons, that is, a "co-city." A co-city should be based on collaborative governance of the commons whereby urban, environmental, cultural, knowledge, and digital commons are comanaged by the five actors of the collaborative/polycentric governance—social innovators (i.e., active citizens, makers, digital innovators, urban regenerators, rurban innovators, etc.), public authorities, businesses, civil society organizations, and knowledge institutions (i.e., schools, universities, cultural academies, etc.)—through an institutionalized public-private-citizen partnership. This partnership, pioneered in Italy, will give birth to a local peer-to-peer physical, digital, and institutional platform with three main aims: living together (collaborative services), growing together (co-ventures), making together (co-production). The project is supported by the local Chamber of Commerce, the City, the Province, local NGOs, young entrepreneurs, SMEs, and knowledge institutions, such as the Mantua University Foundation, and some very forward-looking local schools.[18]

This project, launched by the Laboratory for the Governance of Commons (LabGov) of Bologna, resembles the longstanding tradition of cooperatives in Italy, which feels odd in a world dominated by corporations. If we take a closer look at recent research, however, the latter is not so strange after all. The emergence and formalization of cooperative organizational forms that basically rely on sharing activities most commonly occur when the corporations represent a potential threat to the autonomy of the local economy, leading to a generally anticorporate climate, and there is a well-established organizational infrastructure supporting a cooperative ideology.[19] This is also more likely to occur in Europe than in North America.

The confluence of factors discussed in the early part of this book, such as the emergence of the sharing economy, civic entrepreneurs, and ubiquitous and cheap technologies, is supporting the potential for urban commons. This makes us wonder what if our cities were treated as urban commons whereby all stakeholders had more of an equal share of responsibility and autonomy to enact improvements in our urban environment? What if the role of city government was to facilitate or enable civic entrepreneurs, citizens, and other stakeholders to develop policy and even to conceive of, finance, and develop new infrastructure?

## SEEMS THAT WE ARE NOT THAT CRAZY AFTER ALL

For these reasons and many others including cultural factors, the United States seems to be losing its stranglehold as top innovator. In fact there is credible evidence that the United States is not even close to being number one in the world in innovation already, and a potentially "new normal" lower rate of entrepreneurship activity has emerged following the Great Recession.[20]

The Global Innovation Index is an annual ranking of innovation capabilities and results in countries around the globe developed by Cornell University, INSEAD, and the World Intellectual Property Organization of the United Nations. The Global Innovation Index is comprised of seven pillars (institutions, human capital and research, infrastructure, market sophistication, business sophistication, knowledge and technology outputs, and creative outputs). In order to assess countries on those seven pillars, the research team collects data on 81 indicators. The 2014 index is quite telling. The United States does not even make the top five! Switzerland, United Kingdom, Sweden, Finland, and the Netherlands all beat out the United States, which landed in the sixth place. Rounding out the top 10 are Singapore, Denmark, Luxembourg, and Hong Kong (China).

While the Global Innovation Index focuses on ranking innovation at the country level, 2Thinknow, a private consultancy, has been conducting a Global Innovation Cities Index every year since 2007. The 2Thinknow team currently ranks 445 cities around the world using 162 indicators to assess how innovative each city's economy is. While the results do not exactly mirror those of the Global Innovation Index, there are certainly similarities with respect to the diversity of countries represented in the top of the leadership board. For example, in their 2014 ranking only 5 of the top 20 cities are in the United States (San Francisco (1), New York (2), Boston (4), Seattle (10), Los Angeles (14). Europe actually has 10 cities in the top 20, double that of the United States. Tops in Europe include London (3), Paris (5), Vienna (6), Munich (7), Amsterdam (8), Copenhagen (9), Berlin (13), Stockholm (16), Hamburg (18), and Lyon (19). The only cities outside of the United States and Europe to make the top 20 include: Toronto (11), Seoul (12), Tokyo (15), Sydney (17), and Hong Kong (20).

From 2011 to 2014, Boyd has been leading annual rankings of smart cities in different regions around the globe and published the results in Fast Company. The rankings were based on the smart cities wheel and initially 28 indicators and later 62 indicators. Because of issues with data comparability, he only ranks cities on a regional basis (i.e., North America, Latin America, Europe, and Asia/Pacific). However, what the ranking reveals is that European cities are leading the pack. As he considers innovation in everything from procurement practices and sustainability to mobility and smarter government (e.g., online services, mobile app development), it is not surprising that the results and analysis are consistent with those of the Global Innovation Cities Index.

The democratization of innovation, combined with declining costs and shared access to technology resources, the decreased dependence on venture capital for early-stage financing, and the growing desire for the creative class to live in vibrant, walkable urban cities, is changing the landscape of entrepreneurship and innovation the world over. Quality of life, good public transit, culture, leisure time, and open spaces are high priorities for many of the millennials, and in general, European cities score higher in these areas. Cities in California, Texas, and their siblings are not precisely walkable nor overflowing with public spaces (no, shopping malls do not count).

In early 2016, Boyd had the chance to sit down with Antoni Brey, the founder of Urbiotica, a Barcelona-based smart cities/Internet of Things startup. In the wide-ranging interview one topic clearly caught Boyd's attention. It turns out that in 2011, Brey was looking at Urbiotica's growth plans and was seriously considering relocating the company to Silicon Valley. Yet as Brey conducted several meetings with interested venture capitalists and other players in the entrepreneurial ecosystem, he was struck by the realization that there may be no benefit, and in fact, a move to the Valley could be detrimental to Urbiotica's growth. First and foremost, Brey explained, Urbiotica's end user are cities, who have long decision-making cycles, not conducive to the growth rates expected by venture capitalists. Furthermore, he continued, costs of living and quality of life in the Valley are not nearly as competitive as they are in Barcelona. In fact many entrepreneurs he spoke with said why would you want to move from Barcelona to live here? We'd prefer to live in Barcelona ourselves! While this is only anecdotal it serves to reinforce several arguments Boyd made earlier in this book regarding the potentially decreased dependence on venture capital and the increased attention entrepreneurs pay to quality of life and walkability.

This is one reason we believe we will see a continuing shift of power in the innovation and entrepreneurship landscape toward Europe. In Mercer's annual ranking of quality of life in cities around the globe, European cities shine. Thirteen of the top 20 cities in the 2015 ranking are European. In fact the first North American city on the list is Vancouver at number 5 and the first U.S. city is San Francisco at number 27! If the allure of Silicon Valley is declining, even among Bay Area founders, then perhaps more European entrepreneurs will dream big and locate in a top European city.

The open democratization of innovation and entrepreneurship in the recent decades has changed the dynamics and permits cities outside of the United States to become competitive if they can offer other benefits that the current generation of entrepreneurs values. Also, it is much cheaper and easier for cities to support the creation of the invisible infrastructure that supports these ecosystems. And again, in this arena, we feel that Europe is already taking the lead. Take, for example, Fab Labs, which we discussed in previous chapters. Despite being the brainchild of Boston-based MIT, the growth in Fab Labs is stronger in Europe than in the United States. At the time of this writing there were less than 100 Fab Labs in the United States but nearly 250 in Europe. Most notably, a great number of those in Europe are either open to or run by the community.

Contrary to what you might be thinking, these are not low-tech venues for assembling Lego blocks; rather, they are advanced workshop spaces for rapid prototyping and computer-based design.

In the somewhat related world of crowdsourcing, we observe similar trends—alongside the rather radical cases of Iceland and Finland. For example, Citymart, an early mover in creating a two-sided platform to connect cities with civic tech innovators around the globe, is not based in the United States but rather Barcelona and Copenhagen, two leading innovative cities in Europe. Note that while Barcelona did not make to the Global Innovation Cities Index top 20 (currently ranked 56th), the city has regularly scored in the top 5 in the smart cities ranking Boyd has been leading for the last few years and was recently named smartest city in the world by Juniper Research[21] and won the 2015 European Capital of Innovation Award as well.

Will we see the next Google come out of a European city or an emerging city from Asia or Latin America? We are not sure. But we will definitely see a growing number of successful urban entrepreneurs based in cities outside of Silicon Valley, Boston, and New York, who are competing on a world stage. Steve Case, AOL's founder and start-up investor via Revolution Ventures, appears to agree:

Most of the attention and most of the capital still finds its way to places like Silicon Valley and Boston and New York City, but there are great companies and thriving start-up communities being built all across the country. The story of American entrepreneurship in other parts of the country, and in sectors other than technology, just isn't being told, and that has to change.[22]

Back to Europe. Between 2000 and 2014, 30 tech companies were founded in the region that had valuations in excess of $1 billion.[23] Manish Madhvani, cofounder of GP Bullhound, is bullish on Europe:

Europe is much more adept at creating billion-dollar tech companies than most experts expected. The fact that it is in touching distance of the US demonstrates how both the ambition levels and ecosystem have progressed to allow entrepreneurs to scale global businesses.[24]

We realize our opinion that European cities and the continent as a whole may be better positioned for modern innovation and entrepreneurship opportunities is certainly controversial. It also flies in the face of history and current economic trends. As we write this chapter, the dollar is on track to reach parity with the Euro for the first time in 10 years, and some are predicting the dollar will be stronger than the Euro in the coming years. The U.S. economy on paper is stronger than Europe's and is not facing potential default and bailouts in countries that have been faced with significant austerity measures and resulting unrest like that of Greece and even Spain. Time will tell and history may prove that we have a few screws loose. But we are bullish on Europe's potential in the coming decades to become a more important player on the global entrepreneurship and innovation scene than the United States.

## THE FUTURE OF THE URBANPRENEUR SPIRAL, NEW COLLISIONS

Three forces sustain our model today. Can we expect to see new forces emerging in the future? If so, will they be leading to new collisions? Guess what, we do not have the answer either. But we can draw some lines into the future looking at today's trends.

### Urbanization Force in the Coming Decades

We do think that new forces may emerge in the years to come. Certainly cities will continue growing, but with that perhaps we will see an atomization as large urban areas decentralize into a collection of small neighborhoods with their own identity, culture, and social life, contrary to the spreading of satellite neighborhoods in suburban areas we have witnessed in the past. Just like communities in Europe such as Catalunya and Pais Vasco have raised their voice claiming independence from the central government, it is likely we will see smart neighborhoods initiating dialogues with local councils toward higher autonomy when it comes to specific matters such as energy efficiency, waste management, carbon emissions, and alike. Nesta's neighborhood challenge fostered this in a sense. Through social experimenting, it brought decision-making and power back to the communities so they can resolve their own specific problems. When neighborhoods realize that they have the right tools and power in their hands to improve their circumstances, they get together to create innovative responses to local priorities. The end result is that, together with solving the problem, social capital is created leading to the (re)emergence of an identity and culture rooted in the neighborhood's characteristics. Based on our own research[25] and observations, we expect to see urban entrepreneurs leading community organizations and playing a catalytic role in the space, prompting further the atomization of cities.

An example of the latter is the emergence of organizations that are somehow pursuing this trend. Inspired Neighborhoods (IN), for example, is a community interest company in the UK that supports communities and businesses in Bradford in community-led regeneration activities and independent neighborhood management. It is the small version of the city-wide civic platforms Boyd has mentioned throughout the book. Inspired Neighborhoods seeks to foster inclusive, just and prosperous neighborhoods by empowering people to influence decisions that affect their lives.

with imagination and determination, communities can develop new thinking which will produce prosperity and diversity by being integrated into networks of trust and commitment. It aims to create a society which acknowledges the imperative of sharing risk and wealth, thus narrowing the gap between neighbourhoods.[26]

Two hours south from Bradford, in north London, the Walthamstow community launched not long ago a volunteer-led hub to supporting neighborhood-led projects. The Mill opened in 2012 as whole-community venture after a campaign to keep the St James Street Library open. The campaign was successful, with a group of residents taking over the lease of the library and establishing this self-running community space.

Back in the Yorkshire, the Bradford Moor Neighborhood is investing in local social entrepreneurs to kickstart neighborhood-led change. Changemakers in Manchester, Lower Green in Surrey, Coopers edge trust in Gloucestershire, SE-village in Peckham, and the list continues. Nesta's experiment led to interesting findings. They found five factors that enable locally led innovation and change: relationships need to be based on a strong, locally-led vision for change; experimentation and risk-taking is to be encouraged in order to find new ways of engaging people; communities require more flexible ways to contract with and monitor groups, reflecting local variety; a supportive funding environment that is conducive to enabling change is in place; and a learning culture exists in the community.

As these factors continue to grow and gain traction in local communities, with more and more urbanpreneurs leading for change, neighborhood-led innovation will continue on the raise and will eventually emerge as a fourth force alongside urbanization, democratization, and collaboration.

## Collaboration Force in the Coming Decades

Without a doubt we will continue to see multinational companies, cities, start-ups, citizen groups, universities, and others continue to collaborate on projects, like the AMS Institute in Amsterdam, in hopes of finding innovative solutions, and new business models, to make cities more sustainable and livable. Furthermore, we do not feel it is possible to understate the potential ramifications and permutations of collaborative models going forward. We are potentially at a critical juncture of the global economy. Cities already are driving the global economy. As discussed in previous chapters, 600 of the world's cities, representing just 22 percent of the world's population, already account for 60 percent of global GDP. Cities are also largely responsible for much of the world's pollution, waste, energy consumption, and carbon emissions. Cities are a major part of the environmental crisis the world is facing but are also the potential source of the solution. Aside from greener buildings and energy, better waste and reuse strategies, and so on, the collaborative (or sharing) economy may be an absolutely critical component of making cities, and the globe, more sustainable. The take-make-waste society of the Industrial Revolution almost certainly needs to give way to a more circular economy where resources remain in use and circulation and where we, as a society, are better at optimizing subutilized resources.

And no, we don't mean that we need more traditional capitalism masked as sharing economy, like Uber, but rather we expect, and hope, the cities will be the birth of economic and noneconomic sharing models that will allow a more efficient use of finite global resources. As far as we are aware, there is only one planet that has been proven to be inhabitable by humans, and that is planet Earth. If we are to retain, or even improve quality of life for the growing global and urban population, cities and urbanpreneurs must lead us into a more sustainable, circular, and sharing economy. While some of the solutions will certainly rely on technology and virtual platforms, others may be decidedly low-tech and local. The Repair Cafés popping up around the globe are one such example. In Barcelona, on Tuesdays residents are allowed to place unwanted furniture on the street so that others who discover the undervalued nightstand, sofa, or chair can make use of it, rather than sending it to the landfill. Time banks, like the one offered by Bliive mentioned above, are another, noneconomic approach to sharing we expect to see growing in the future. Aside from the environmental benefits of true sharing, which must necessarily include the optimization of subutilized resources, the type of sharing discussed here also has the potential to raise the quality of life for lower-income urban residents by allowing them access to things, services, and even income they otherwise would not have had access to.

We will see a continued growth of the sharing economy and, in fact, we believe, an explosion of new sharing economy models, particularly in cities. These sharing models will not only be introduced by urbpanpreneurs and global start-ups but corporations will continue to engage in the sharing economy. It is often better to cannibalize a company's traditional business model with a new product or service line than wait for it to be entirely disrupted and eventually disappear as new, better, more efficient, and cost-effective services emerge. BMW has recognized this. They are aware that the younger generation cares more about having a smartphone and a good data plan than owning their own vehicles. Rather than wait for millennials to reach maturity and continue to avoid purchasing their own vehicles, BMW decided to jump in and participate in the sharing economy by launching Drive Now, an electric vehicle carsharing program in several cities around the globe. While it may reduce the demand for new vehicles, it also exposes the brand to potential future customers, and even if they never buy a BMW, the company has found a new way to generate revenue from customers who otherwise would have never purchased one of their vehicles.

Furthermore, the likely ubiquity of the sharing economy going forward will necessarily result in a further segmentation of the sharing economy. There will be new categories of sharing, some of which will be very profit driven and really just represent a different service delivery model. Others will be more altruistic, like Repair Cafés, or even initiatives like that of Patagonia who have encouraged customers to not buy new Patagonia gear and instead acquire used Patagonia gear through a collaboration with Amazon.com. What we are saying is that to date, most of the conversations about the sharing economy have sought to paint all sharing activity with the same brush. In the near future, we expect consumers, citizens, companies, and start-ups will begin to create even more divergence within the sharing economy, not just which sectors like shared space, logistics, transportation, and so on but also the underlying motivation, business model, and social benefit offered by the service. We truly believe the future is very bright for the sharing economy and that the growing diversity of business models and approaches will mostly be beneficial to society and to our cities.

## Democratization Force in the Coming Decades

In the first chapter of this book we provided a quote from Austin Smith in *Venture Beat* about how the cost of bringing a tech solution to the market has gone from $2.5 million to $250,000 to just $250 today. We are not going to say that it will reduce to $25 although it could, or almost go to free with someone smart enough to leverage the sharing economy to provide a unique combination of resources, to deliver value. But what we do believe, and sincerely hope, is that the tools for innovation will continue to diffuse, not only in cities around the globe but to all income and education levels. Pablo and Boyd have both spent a lot of time in countries and communities in the developing world where we have witnessed first-hand how the base of the pyramid lives (i.e., the lower income levels of the 99 percent). The digital divide, which still exists today, especially in developing countries, poses a significant challenge for income equality and opportunity in cities and rural areas around the globe. If cities can help bring STEM, STEAM, and E(STEAM) education into the classrooms of all public schools, this will provide an invaluable contribution toward closing the digital divide and enabling all income levels to participate in the future economy. Also the tools of innovation in the future, things like 3D Printers, Fab Labs, online networks of users, and collaborators, need to become ubiquitous and accessible to all. This is not just an altruistic concern we have about the world's poor. The more cities are able to provide inclusivity, the better they function. The winner-take-all urbanism discussed by Florida in his latest book doesn't benefit anyone, even the "winners" in the end. Societies with greater income inequality function worse than those with lower levels. High levels of income inequality (often measured via the Gini index) have more problems with crime, unemployment, and health levels, which in return place higher burdens on tax payers and cities to provide for the basic needs of people who are unable to do so for themselves.

Nick Hanauer, a billionaire who has invested in some of the most important tech start-ups in the United States, has recognized how income inequality leads to disfunction in his home city of Seattle. So he spearheaded the U.S. first effort to develop a truly livable minimum wage of $15 per hour for all employees working in the city. In a series of impassioned articles and speeches, Hanauer managed to convince several public officials, including those in Seattle, to embrace the $15 per hour minimum wage. In a scathing critique of "trickle down economics" models, Hanauer has suggested that

when workers have more money, businesses have more customers, they hire more workers. And when fast-food restaurants pay workers enough so that even they can afford to eat the food they serve, that isn't bad for the fast-food business, it is great for it, despite what McDonald's and other sin the fast-food industry will tell you. Living wages in the fast-food industry are simply good for business.[27]

You may be asking, what does this living wage thing have to do with urbanpreneurship. Those making a living wage have a better chance to participate in the urban economy, buy or access local products and services, and perhaps even become future urbanpreneurs because they will be better able to access education and innovation opportunities.

### Citizens, Cities, and Urbanpreneurs Going Forward

Throughout this book we have highlighted the urbanization trends occurring throughout the globe and the challenges cities will continue to face as billions more migrate to cities in the hopes of better opportunities and quality of life. What future will these new migrants face will increasingly depend more on themselves and their fellow citizens than local governments. City administrators will not have enough financial resources, or sufficient capacity to innovate, in order to maintain and improve the basic and growing needs of the urban masses. Not only will citizens expect access to jobs, quality education, fantastic transit, a clean environment, green spaces, reliable energy, and organic and local food, but, as Boyd's friend Pablo Sanchez Chillon has suggested, citizens are becoming digizens.

City residents are becoming more digitally enabled "digizens" and demanding more services, on demand, in real time, and location based from their cities. But the old paradigm of one-way service deliver from bureaucratic city administrations to the masses is rapidly giving way to a new model of citizen engagement, civic hackers, and urbanpreneurs. This is a good thing too. While embracing open innovation and citizen and private sector involvement in the delivery of services and infrastructure might be scary for cities, it also opens up the prospect for a better future for cities, and their residents and visitors. We are convinced the coming decades will be full of even further rapid adoption of innovation, smarter cities, and a growth in the numbers and types of urbanpreneurs seeking to leverage the urban infrastructure, hard and soft, to not only generate income for themselves but also improve the quality of lives for their neighbors and global colleagues. The race is on for cities to attract and retain the innovators of the future and hopefully this book provides insights for those innovators and the cities who hope to seduce them.

# Notes

## FOREWORD

1. Fred Wilson, "Cause and Effect," July 2012. http://avc.com/2012/07/cause-effect/

## CHAPTER 1

1. R. G. Lipsey, K. I. Carlaw, & C. T. Bekar, 2005. *Economic Transformations: General Purpose Technologies and Long-Term Economic Growth*. Oxford University Press, page 5.

2. J. Yarow, "Apple Is Spending $200 million a Year Fighting Android Patent Lawsuits around the World," *Business Insider*, November 14, 2013. http://www.businessinsider.com/apple-is-spending-200-million-a-year-fighting-android-patent-lawsuits-2013-11

3. C. Duhigg & S. Lohr, "The Patent, Used as a Sword," *New York Times*, October 7, 2012. http://www.nytimes.com/2012/10/08/technology/patent-wars-among-tech-giants-can-stifle-competition.html?pagewanted=all

4. D. Hansson, "Reconsider," *Signal v. Noise*, November 5, 2015.

5. D. Mulcahy, B. Weeks, & H. Bradley, "We Have Met the Enemy and the Enemy Is Us: Lessons from Twenty Years of the Kauffman Foundation's Investments in Venture Capital Funds and the Triumph of Hope over Experience," Kauffman Foundation, May 2012. http://www.kauffman.org/~/media/kauffman_org/research%20reports%20and%20covers/2012/05/we_have_met_the_enemy_and_he_is_us.pdf

6. Kauffman Foundation, "Entrepreneurship Education Comes of Age on Campus: The Challenges and Rewards of Bringing Entrepreneurship to Higher Education. 2013." http://www.kauffman.org/~/media/kauffman_org/research%20reports%20and%20covers/2013/08/eshipedcomesofage_report.pdf

7. Pablo Martin de Holan, "The Bitter Truth about Entrepreneurial Success," *Financial Times*, December 21, 2014. http://www.ft.com/cms/s/2/09482d80-637b -11e4-8a63-00144feabdc0.html#axzz3lFJ58h8G

8. *Time*, "The 10 Biggest Tech Failures of the Last Decade," May 14, 2009. http://content.time.com/time/specials/packages/completelist/0,29569, 1898610,00.html

9. F. Alvaredo, A. Atkinson, T. Piketty, & E. Saez, 2013. "The Top 1 Percent in International and Historical Perspectives," *Journal of Economic Perspectives*, 27(3), 3–20. http://pubs.aeaweb.org/doi/pdfplus/10.1257/jep.27.3.3

10. G. Arnett, "The Scale of the Volkswagen Crisis—in Charts," *The Guardian*, September 22, 2015. http://www.theguardian.com/news/datablog/ 2015/sep/22/scale-of-volkswagen-crisis-in-charts

11. A. Petroff, "Volkswagen Scandal May Cost up to $87 Billion," CNN, October 2, 2015. http://money.cnn.com/2015/10/02/news/companies/ volkswagen-scandal-bp-credit-suisse/

12. M. Scott, "Sustainability Now Key Selling Point for Business Schools Attracting Students," *The Guardian*, February 9, 2015. http://www.theguardian .com/sustainable-business/2015/feb/09/are-business-schools-taking-sustainability -seriously

13. T. Teodorczuk, "US Mayors Unveil New Figures on Economic Growth," *Cities Today*, June 21, 2015. http://cities-today.com/us-mayors-unveil-new -research-showing-revival-of-us-cities/

14. S. Brand, "City Planet," Strategy+Business, February, 28, 2006. http:// www.strategy-business.com/article/06109?gko=122db

15. B. Cortright, "Young and Restless," *City Reports*, October 19, 2014. http:// cityobservatory.org/ynr/

16. http://blog.pitchbook.com/what-percentage-of-u-s-vc-backed-startups -are-founded-by-women/

17. "Apple's App Store Generated over $10 Billion in Revenue for Developers in Record 2014," Apple Insider, January 8, 2015. http://appleinsider.com/articles/ 15/01/08/apples-app-store-generated-over-10-billion-in-revenue-for-developers-in -record-2014

18. http://www.teslamotors.com/blog/all-our-patent-are-belong-you

19. P. Moser, 2013. "Patents and Innovation: Evidence from Economic History," *Journal of Economic Perspectives*, 27(1): 23–44.

20. http://www.statista.com/statistics/218601/global-number-of-private-hotspots -since-2009/

21. B. Burch, "FCC Commissioner Visits with Local Entrepreneurs," Startland, July 6, 2015. http://www.startlandnews.com/2015/07/fcc-commissioner -visits-with-local-entrepreneurs/

22. A. Smith, "Here's What Entrepreneurship 3.0 Looks Like," *Venture Beat*, March 1, 2015. http://venturebeat.com/2015/03/01/heres-what-entrepreneurship -3-0-looks-like/

23. M. Nager, "White Paper: Announcing 5 Ingredients for 'Fostering a Thriving Starting Ecosystem,'" Up Global, September 8, 2014. http://blog.up.co/2014/09/08/white-paper-announcing-5-ingredients-fostering-thriving-startup-ecosystem/

24. R. Swart, "World Bank: Crowdfunding Investment Market to Hit $93 Billion by 2025." http://www.pbs.org/mediashift/2013/12/world-bank-crowdfunding-investment-market-to-hit-93-billion-by-2025/

25. D. Netburn, "Pebble Smartwatch Raises $4.7 million on Kickstarter Funding Site," *Los Angeles Times*, April 18, 2012. http://www.latimes.com/business/technology/la-fi-tn-pebble-smart-watch-kickstarter-20120418,0,1769291.story

26. http://www.cnbc.com/2015/02/02/pebble-rolls-with-more-than-1m-smartwatch-shipments-report.html

27. D. Marom, A. Robb, & O. Sade, March 10, 2015. "Gender Dynamics in Crowdfunding (Kickstarter): Evidence on Entrepreneurs, Investors, Deals and Taste Based Discrimination." http://papers.ssrn.com/sol3/papers.cfm?abstract_id=2442954

28. "Crowdfunding's Potential for the Developing World," World Bank, 2013. http://www.infodev.org/infodev-files/infodev_crowdfunding_study_0.pdf

29. Luis Camarinha-Matos, 2002. Collaborative Business Ecosystems and Virtual Enterprises: IFIP TC5/Wg5.5 Third Working Conference on Infrastructures for Virtual Enterprise.

30. N. M. Dahan, J. P. Doh, J. Oetzel, & M. Yaziji, 2010. "Corporate-NGO Collaboration: Co-creating New Business Models for Developing Markets," *Long Range Planning*, 43(2), 326–342.

31. http://www.credport.org/blog/12-Why-a-Drill-is-a-Bad-Example-for-the-Sharing-Economy

32. R. Winkler & D. Macmillan, "The Secret Math of Airbnb's $24 Billion Valuation," *The Wall Street Journal*, June 17, 2015. http://www.wsj.com/articles/the-secret-math-of-airbnbs-24-billion-valuation-1434568517

33. N. Gorenflo, How Platform Coops Can Beat Death Stars Like Uber to Create a Real Sharing Economy, November 3, 2015, Shareable.net

34. https://medium.com/@bchesky/shared-city-db9746750a3a

35. S. Bertoni, "Rent the Runway Nears End of Series D Round, Valuation Could Top $600 Million," *Forbes*, October 28, 2014. http://www.forbes.com/sites/stevenbertoni/2014/10/28/rent-the-runway-nears-end-of-series-d-round-valuation-could-top-600-million/

36. "The Sharing Economy," Price Waterhouse Coopers, 2015. https://www.pwc.com/us/en/technology/publications/assets/pwc-consumer-intelligence-series-the-sharing-economy.pdf

37. J. Owyang, "How Investors Are Sharing Their Money into the Collaborative Economy," March 17, 2015. http://www.web-strategist.com/blog/2015/03/17/how-investors-are-sharing-their-money-into-the-collaborative-economy/

38. B. Cohen & P. Muñoz, forthcoming. "Sharing Cities and Sustainable Consumption and Production." http://www.web-strategist.com/blog/2015/03/ 17/how-investors-are-sharing-their-money-into-the-collaborative-economy/

## CHAPTER 2

1. T. Kane, "The Importance of Startups in Job Creation and Job Destruction," Kauffman Foundation Research Series, July 2010. http://www .kauffman.org/~/media/kauffman_org/research%20reports%20and%20covers/ 2010/07/firm_formation_importance_of_startups.pdf

2. "The Budget Outlook for the Small Business Administration," April 24, 2013. http://www.gpo.gov/fdsys/pkg/CHRG-113hhrg80822/html/CHRG -113hhrg80822.htm

3. C. Räthke, "Kick Out Bayern Munchen! How Starting at Silicon Valley Distracts Us from the Important Thing," May 3, 2015. https://techberlin.com/ articles/state-berlin-ecosystem-or-bundesliga-171/

4. P. Graham, "How to Be Silicon Valley," May 2006. http://www .paulgraham.com/siliconvalley.html

5. R. Nieva, "Vexed in the City: Silicon Valley's Invasion of San Francisco," CNET, August 22, 2014. http://www.cnet.com/news/vexed-in-the-city-silicon -valleys-invasion-of-san-francisco/

6. Ibid.

7. J. Defterios & A. Chen, "Move Over Silicon Valley, San Francisco Is New Hippest Tech Scene," CNN, February 18, 2015. http://edition.cnn.com/2015/ 02/17/americas/san-francisco-tech-hub/

8. D. Alba, "Uber's Move to Oakland Will Test an Economy in Overdrive," Wired, October 11, 2015. http://www.wired.com/2015/10/uber-moving-to -oakland-will-test-its-economy/

9. Brookings Institution, "The Rise of Innovation Districts: A New Geography of Innovation in America," 2014.

10. "10 Years of 22@: The Innovation District." http://www.22barcelona .com/documentacio/informe_10anys_eng.pdf

11. http://www.carloratti.com/project/medellinnovation-district/

12. Brookings Institution, "The Rise of Innovation Districts."

13. B. Cohen, "The Smartest Cities in the World," Fast Company, November 20, 2014. http://www.fastcoexist.com/3038765/fast-cities/the-smartest -cities-in-the-world

14. V. Mulas, "Does Social Dimension Beat Geographic Clustering in Creating Tech Innovation Ecosystems in Cities," The World Bank, March 19, 2015. http:// blogs.worldbank.org/ic4d/does-social-dimension-beat-geographic-clustering-creating -tech-innovation-ecosystems-cities?cid=EXT_WBBlogSocialShare_D_EXT

15. "Why Kansas City Needs High Collision Density (and How We Can Get It)," Think Big Partners, August 13, 2013. http://thinkbigkansascity.blogspot .com/2013/08/why-kansas-city-needs-high-collision.html

## CHAPTER 3

1. "Tax Revenue Forecasting Documentation: Financial Plan Fiscal Years 2012–2016." http://www.nyc.gov/html/omb/downloads/pdf/methodology_2013_04.pdf

2. Great Cities, Calgary Chamber of Commerce, 2014.

3. Manchester Evening News, "Revealed: 3,172 Salford People Applied for BBC MediaCity Jobs—and Only 24 Were Hired, January 17, 2012." http://www.manchestereveningnews.co.uk/news/greater-manchester-news/revealed-3172-salford-people-applied-679921

4. J. Jacobs, 1961. *The Death and Life of Great American Cities*. New York: Random House.

5. R. Sennett, "The Open City," pages 1–14. https://www.richardsennett.com/site/senn/UploadedResources/The%20Open%20City.pdf

6. "Detroit Leads the Way on Place-Centred Revitalization," Project for Public Spaces, March 25, 2014. http://www.pps.org/projects/detroit-leads-the-way-on-place-centered-revitalization/

7. Susan Sillberberg & Katie Lorrah, 2013. *Places in the Making: How Placemaking Builds Places and Communities*. MIT, DUSP.

8. S. Singer, J. E. Amoras, & D. Moska, "Global Entrepreneurship Monitor," 2014 Global Report, GEM Consortium, 2015. http://www.gemconsortium.org/report/49079

9. "Great North Build Launches New Institute for Social Renewal," Newcastle University Alumni, April 2, 2012. http://www.ncl.ac.uk/alumni/arches/page.htm?new-institute-for-social-renweal-launched-at-newcastle-university-copy1

10. B. Cohen & P. Munoz, 2015. "Toward a Theory of Purpose-Driven Urban Entrepreneurship." *Organization & Environment*. 28(3), 264–285.

11. P. Muñoz and B. Cohen, 2016. "The Making of the Urban Entrepreneur" *California Management Review* (Forthcoming).

12. Majora Carter, urban revitalization strategist, MaArthur Foundation, September 1, 2005. http://www.macfound.org/fellows/753/

13. W. Hu, "Hero of the Bronx Is Now Accused of Betraying It," *New York Times*, April 4, 2013. http://www.nytimes.com/2013/04/05/nyregion/a-hero-of-the-bronx-majora-carter-is-now-accused-of-betraying-it.html?_r=0

14. P. Daugherty, P. Banerjee, W. Negm, & A. Alter, "Driving Unconventional Growth through the Industrial Internet of Things," Accenture Technology, 2015. https://www.accenture.com/mz-en/technology-labs-insight-industrial-internet-of-things.aspx

## CHAPTER 4

1. "Employment Arrangements: Improved Outreach Could Help Ensure Proper Worker Classification," U.S. Government Accountability Office, GAO-06-656. http://www.gao.gov/new.items/d06656.pdf

2. S. Horowitz & F. Rosati, "53 Million Americans Are Freelancing, New Survey Finds," Freelancers Union, September 4, 2014. https://www.freelancers union.org/blog/dispatches/2014/09/04/53million/

3. S. Larson, "The Great Recession Could Happen Again Soon, and This Time It Could Be Worse," *The Street*, October 14, 2015. http://www.thestreet .com/story/13322947/1/the-great-recession-could-happen-again-soon-and-this -time-it-could-be-worse-for-u-s.html

4. "Spain Youth Unemployment Rate, 1986–2015," Trading Economics. http://www.tradingeconomics.com/spain/youth-unemployment-rate

5. R. Smith & C. Mckenna, "Temped Out: How the Domestic Outsourcing of Blue-Collar Jobs Harms America's Workers," National Employment Law Project. http://www.nelp.org/page/-/Reports/Temped-Out.pdf?nocdn=1

6. S. Boyd, "ODesk Spring 2013 Online Work Survey Is Out," GigaOM Research, May 14, 2013. http://research.gigaom.com/2013/05/odesk-spring -2013-online-work-survey-is-out//

7. T. M. Obser, "Why Soft Infrastructure Is Key to Shaping Dynamic New Cities," New Cities Foundation, April 1, 2015. http://www.newcitiesfoundation .org/why-soft-infrastructure-is-key-to-shaping-dynamic-new-cities/

8. C. Landry & F. Bianchini, 1995. *The Creative City*, page 22. Demos.

9. "Supporting Places of Work: Incubators, Accelerators and Co-working Spaces, Greater London Authority," 2014. https://www.london.gov.uk/priorities/ regeneration/publications-guidance/supporting-places-of-work-incubators -accelerators-and-co-working

10. B. Waber, J. Magnolfi, & G. Lindsay, "Workspaces That Move People," *Harvard Business Review*, October 2014. https://hbr.org/2014/10/workspaces -that-move-people

11. E. Fletcher, "Co-work Spaces after Landscape for Entrepreneurs," The Modesto Bee, February 21, 2015. http://www.modbee.com/news/article10910489 .html

12. "Coworking Forecast: 1 Million Coworkers in 2018," Small Business Labs, May 7, 2014. http://www.smallbizlabs.com/2014/05/coworking-forecast.html

13. http://www.ideascartel.com/

14. GoToLaunch, "Top 3 Co-Working Spaces for Technology Entrepreneurs in Bali," e27, April 2, 2015. http://e27.co/top-3-co-working-spaces-technology -entrepreneurs-bali-20150402/

15. T. Rogers, "Berlin Is the Post-Tourist Capital of Europe," *New York Magazine*, May 17, 2015. http://nymag.com/next/2015/03/berlin-is-the-post -tourist-capital-of-europe.html#

16. C. O'Brien, "Princeton Economist Explains Why We Should All Stop Worrying and Learn to Love Uber," *Venture Beat*, January 22, 2015. http:// venturebeat.com/2015/01/22/inside-ubers-staggering-u-s-growth-40000-drivers -joined-in-december-and-average-19-per-hour/

17. F. Manjoo, "Uber, a Rising Business Model That Could Change How You Work," *New York Times*, January 28, 2015. http://www.nytimes.com/2015/01/29/

technology/personaltech/uber-a-rising-business-model.html?smid=tw-share
&_r=5

18. J. Chaney, "Shenzhen: China's Start-Up City Defies Skeptics," CNN, June 24, 2015. http://edition.cnn.com/2015/05/14/tech/shenzhen-startup-city/index.html

19. http://www.adafruit.com/faq

20. J. Novet, "Etsy Raises $267M in IPO at $16 Per Share," *Venture Beat*, April 15, 2015. http://venturebeat.com/2015/04/15/etsy-is-reportedly-raising-267m-in-ipo-with-stock-going-for-16-per-share/

21. S. Gandel, "This Is the Worst Performing IPO of 2015." http://fortune.com/2015/06/08/etsy-ipo-worst-2015/

22. http://www.fabfoundation.org/about-us/

23. E. Siemasko, "Building a Freelance Career? Hera Are the 5 Best Cities to Live In," Skyword, February 9, 2015. http://www.skyword.com/contentstandard/for-storytellers/building-a-freelance-career-here-are-the-5-best-cities-to-live-in/

24. M. Chafkin, "And the Money Comes Rolling in, Inc., January 1, 2009." http://www.inc.com/magazine/20090101/and-the-money-comes-rolling-in.html

25. M. Rivas, "Innovative Place Brand Management: Re-learning City Branding," Urbact, 2015. http://urbact.eu/sites/default/files/final_report_urbact_citylogo_2012-2015_miguel_rivas.pdf

26. "Supporting Places of Work: Incubators, Accelerators and Co-working Spaces," Greater London Authority, 2014. https://www.london.gov.uk/priorities/regeneration/publications-guidance/supporting-places-of-work-incubators-accelerators-and-co-working

27. C. Dewey & Ryan Gepper, "Inventor of the 'Coolest Cooler', Failed Many Times before Raising $13 million on Kickstarter," *Washington Post*, August 28, 2014. https://www.washingtonpost.com/news/the-intersect/wp/2014/08/28/ryan-grepper-inventor-of-the-coolest-cooler-failed-many-times-before-raising-11-million-on-kickstarter/

## CHAPTER 5

1. M. Chitty, "The Purpose of a City: Economic Development or Something More," January 27, 2012. https://leedscd.wordpress.com/2012/01/27/the-purpose-of-a-city-economic-development-or-something-more/

2. G. Oliver, "EU Meddling Could Cost Us Thousands Every Year, Warn UK's Online Sewing and Craft Entrepreneurs Fighting the VAT Mess." http://www.thisismoney.co.uk/money/smallbusiness/article-3028585/EU-VAT-mess-hits-online-sewing-craft-entrepreneurs.html

3. D. Raths, "Will the Chief Innovation Officer Transform Government? Government Technology," January 31, 2013. http://www.govtech.com/e-government/Will-the-Chief-Innovation-Officer-Transform-Government.html

4. http://www.covenantofmayors.eu/about/covenant-of-mayors_en.html

5. J. Wingrove, "Edmonton Looks for Cash in Its Trash," The Globe and Mail, January 8, 2013. http://www.theglobeandmail.com/news/national/edmonton-looks-for-cash-in-its-trash/article7073602/

6. "Ayuntament de Barcelona, 10 Years of 22@: The Innovation District," 2011. http://www.22barcelona.com/10x22barcelona/wp-content/uploads/2011/01/informe_10anys_en.pdf

7. http://www.firstlegoleague.org/mission/founders

8. President Obama in his 2013 State of the Union Address.

9. Brookings Institution, "The Rise of Innovation Districts: A New Geography of Innovation in America," 2014, page 4.

10. S. Sims, B. Wilson, & J. Tyrrell, "This Is for Everyone: Connecting Young People and the Tech City," Centre for London, March 2015. http://centreforlondon.org/wp-content/uploads/2015/05/CFL_THIS_IS_FOR_EVERYONE_REPORT.pdf

11. Brookings Institution, "The Rise of Innovation Districts."

12. Mayor's Press Office, "Mayor Walsh Announces the Neighborhood Innovation District Committee," September 26, 2014. http://www.cityofboston.gov/news/Default.aspx?id=14817

13. D. Murali, "Citizen Engagement in City's Policy-Making," The Hindu, November 6, 2010. http://www.thehindu.com/books/citizen-engagement-in-citys-policymaking/article871014.ece

14. "Mayor of London's Office Launches 'Smart Cities' Competition," GreenWise, January 26, 2015. http://www.greenwisebusiness.co.uk/news/mayor-of-londons-office-launches-smart-cities-competition-4528.aspx#.VSWDrSiizSH

15. ENOLL, "Membership Application, ENOLL 6th Wave," European Network of Living Labs. http://www.openlivinglabs.eu/sites/enoll.org/files/042_ENOLL_6W_E_Santander.pdf

16. http://www.ams-amsterdam.com

17. http://kcmayor.org/mayors-agenda-items/innovation-partnership-program

18. B. Burch, "RFP365 Partners with Kansas City, Raises $950k," Startland, May 1, 2015. http://www.startlandnews.com/2015/05/frfp365-partners-with-kansas-city-raises-950k/

19. http://edckc.com/business-solutions/kc-start-up-scene/

20. Private conversations with Aaron Deacon in 2015.

21. http://www.adelaidecitycouncil.com/your-community/library-services/digital-spaces/media-lab/

22. "Checked Out," Economist, December 3, 2011. http://www.economist.com/node/21541063

23. E. Clarence, "Cohesive or Corrosive? Why the Sharing Economy Is Dividing Cities," UrbAct, April 13, 2015. http://urbact.eu/cohesive-or-corrosive-why-sharing-economy-dividing-cities

24. "Portland Private For-Hire Transportation Task Force Report to City Council," April 9, 2015. https://www.portlandoregon.gov/transportation/66552

25. Private discussions with April Rinne in 2015.

## CHAPTER 6

1. J. Mulder, "Minnesota's Small-Towns: A Tour of a Crisis in the Making," *Star Tribune*, March 7, 2014. http://www.startribune.com/opinion/commentaries/249068521.html

2. Bruce Katz, "An Innovation District Grows in Chattanooga," The Brookings Institution, September 29, 2015. http://www.brookings.edu/blogs/the-avenue/posts/2015/09/29-innovation-district-chattanooga-katz

3. http://ouishare.net/fr/projects/sharitories

4. http://mayorschallenge.bloomberg.org/index.cfm?objectid=88E27CD0-BF20-11E3-B2360050569A3ED0

5. Kevin Mackey in a private conversation with the author on July 10, 2015.

6. A. M. Peredo & J. Chrisman, 2013. "Toward a Theory of Community-Based Enterprise," *Academy of Management Review*, 31(2), 310.

7. P. Kando, "Modeling a Cooperative Energy Future," *New Main Times*, December 3, 2013. http://www.newmainetimes.org/articles/2013/12/03/modeling-cooperative-energy-future/

8. Jonathan Kestenbaum, chief executive of Nesta.

9. P. Ockerl, "Between Bottom-Up Regeneration and Coworking," March 12, 2015. http://www.blog.urbact.eu/2015/03/between-bottom-up-regeneration-and-coworking/

10. http://stackoverflow.com/research/developer-survey-2015#work-compensation-remote

11. S. O'Brien, "How Etsy's IPO Could Save Cities," CNN, March 11, 2015. http://money.cnn.com/2015/03/11/smallbusiness/etsy-b-corporation-ipo/

12. E. Jaffe, "Why Big Cities Promote Less Innovation Than They Once Did," *Atlantic*, City Lab, February 16, 2015. http://www.citylab.com/work/2015/02/why-big-cities-promote-less-innovation-than-they-once-did/385535/

## CHAPTER 7

1. http://www.theguardian.com/cities/gentrification

2. J. P. Catungal, D. Leslie, & Y. Hii, 2009. "Geographies of Displacement in the Creative City: The Case of Liberty Village, Toronto," *Urban Studies*, 46(5–6), 1095–1114 (quote from page 1111).

3. R. Atkinson & H. Easthope, 2009. "The Consequences of the Creative Class: The Pursuit of Creativity Strategies in Australia's Cities," *International Journal of Urban and Regional Research*, 33(1), 64–79.

4. http://dirt.asla.org/2014/09/26/is-urban-revitalization-without-gentrification-possible/

5. R. Florida, "The New Urban Crisis. Confidential Preview Edition," dated August 2015, page 65.

6. http://blogs.elpais.com/trans-iberian/2014/07/a-take-on-airbnb-in-barcelona.html

7. http://www.telegraph.co.uk/news/worldnews/southamerica/colombia/11058550/How-Popeye-became-Pablo-Escobars-favourite-hitman.html

8. http://www.saferspaces.org.za/blog/entry/learning-from-medellin-a-success-story-of-holistic-violence-prevention

9. http://recollective.ca/projects/vancouver-olympic-village/

10. S. P. Fraiberger & A. Sundararajan, 2015. "Peer-to-Peer Rental Markets in the Sharing Economy," NYU Stern School of Business Research Paper.

11. A. Rinne, "3 Lessons on Financial Inclusion and the Sharing Economy," *Huffington Post*, October 25, 2014. http://www.huffingtonpost.com/april-rinne/three-lessons-on-financia_b_6044312.html

12. B. Cohen & P. Munoz, 2016. "Sharing Cities and Sustainable Consumption and Production: Towards an Integrated Framework," *Journal of Cleaner Production*, in press.

13. Ibid.

14. http://www.bbc.com/news/technology-33364565

15. M. J. Rowley, "Civic Hacking and the Maker Movement Create Smart Cities." The Toolbox. https://www.thetoolbox.org/articles/2241-civic-hacking-and-the-maker-movement-create-smarter-cities?utm_content=bufferef7c6&utm_medium=social&utm_source=twitter.com&utm_campaign=buffer#.VhVeENb_-uV

16. http://nvca.org/pressreleases/annual-venture-capital-investment-tops-48-billion-2014-reaching-highest-level-decade-according-moneytree-report/

17. http://cordis.europa.eu/news/rcn/123217_en.html

18. http://www.shareable.net/blog/interviewed-professor-christian-iaione-on-the-city-as-commons

19. C. Boone & S. Ozcan, 2014. "Why Do Cooperatives Emerge in a World Dominated by Corporations? The Diffusion of Cooperatives in the U.S. Bio-Ethanol Industry, 1978–2013," *Academy of Management Journal*, 57(4), 990–1012.

20. R. Simon & J. Shoulak, "Level of New U.S. Startups Has Stalled," *Wall Street Journal*, October 14, 2015. http://www.wsj.com/articles/level-of-new-u-s-startups-has-stalled-1444869569

21. http://www.juniperresearch.com/press/press-releases/barcelona-named-global-smart-city-2015

22. http://www.washingtonpost.com/news/on-small-business/wp/2015/04/03/with-a-bus-and-a-checkbook-steve-case-tries-to-remap-american-entrepreneurship/

23. http://www.gpbullhound.com

24. http://www.theguardian.com/business/2014/jun/15/billion-dollar-technology-firms-europe-us-asos-zoopla-spotify

25. P. Muñoz & B. Cohen, 2016. "The Making of the Urban Entrepreneur," *California Management Review*, 59(1).

26. http://www.incic.co.uk/index.php/about-us

27. N. Hanauer, "New York Should Raise the Minimum Wage to $15 an Hour," August 12, 2015. http://www.cnbc.com/2015/08/12/billionaire-new-york-should-raise-minimum-wage-to-15-an-hour-commentary.html

# Index

## About the Authors

**Boyd Cohen**, PhD, is professor of entrepreneurship and sustainability at EADA Business School in Barcelona, Spain, and joint professor at the Universitat de Vic. He has published more than two dozen peer-reviewed academic articles on entrepreneurship, sustainability, the sharing economy and smart cities and is the lead guest editor for a special issue of *California Management Review* titled "The City as a Lab: Open Innovation Meets the Collaborative Economy." Cohen is the coauthor of the acclaimed book *Climate Capitalism: Capitalism in the Age of Climate Change* and is a regular contributor to *Fast Company*. Cohen is the founder of the boutique consultancy UrbanInnova and the cofounder of the Sharing Accelerator Barcelona. He received his doctorate in entrepreneurship and strategy from the University of Colorado Boulder.

**Pablo Muñoz**, PhD, is lecturer in business and sustainable change at the Sustainability Research Institute, University of Leeds in the United Kingdom. His research focuses on sustainable entrepreneurship, inclusive innovation, and community enterprising.